Vocabulary

수능단어장

영어동보카 30일 완성 수능단어장

발 행 | 2024년 06월 03일
저 자 | David Na
펴낸이 | 한건희
펴낸곳 | 주식회사 부크크
출판사등록 | 2014.07.15(제2014-16호)
주 소 | 서울특별시 금천구 가산디지털1로 119 SK트윈타워 A동 305호
전 화 | 1670-8316
이메일 | info@bookk.co.kr

ISBN | 979-11-410-8789-0

CONTENTS

CONTENTS

*Vocabulary/Expressions

Day 1

---

occupation [àkjupéiʃən]   직업

- 医 principal activity in your life that you do to earn money
- 동 job, metier, occupancy, profession, vocation
- 예 *men out of occupation*

---

exhibit [igzíbit]   출품하다

- 医 give an exhibition of to an interested audience
- 동 demo, demonstrate, present, show, showcase
- 예 *We will exhibit the new software in Washington*

---

pale [péil]   창백한

- 医 abnormally deficient in color as suggesting physical or emotional distress
- 동 bloodless, mealy, pallid, sallow, wan
- 예 *Her pale face suddenly flushed.*

---

ignore [ignɔ:r]   무시하다

- 医 bar from attention or consideration
- 동 discount, disregard, neglect, overlook, snub
- 예 *She ignored his advances.*

---

assumption [əsʌmpʃən]   가정

- 医 statement that is assumed to be true and from which a conclusion can be drawn
- 동 conjecture, guess, hypothesis, presumption, supposition
- 예 On the assumption that he has been injured we can infer that he will not to play.

---

appear [əpíər]   나타나다

- 医 come into sight or view
- 동 arise, emerge, look, seem, show
- 예 *A new star appeared on the horizon.*

4

cook [kúk]   요리사

图 someone who cooks food

동 baker, chef, culinarian, dough puncher, pastry maker

예 *the [head cook*

---

sprout [spràut]   싹트다

图 produce buds, branches, or germinate

동 bourgeon, germinate, pullulate, shoot, spud

예 *The potatoes sprouted.*

---

mist [míst]   흐려지다

图 make less visible or unclear

동 befog, becloud, cloud, obnubilate, obscure

예 *The stars are misted by the clouds*

---

rent [rént]   임대하다

图 engage for service under a term of contract

동 charter, engage, hire, lease, take

예 *Let's rent a car.*

---

progress [prágrəs]   진보

图 gradual improvement or growth or development

동 advance, development, evolution, headway, improvement

예 *progress of knowledge*

---

lift [líft]   올리다

图 raise from a lower to a higher position

동 arise, elevate, heave, raise, uplift

예 *Lift a load.*

---

precision [prisíʒən]   정확

图 the quality of being reproducible in amount or performance

图 accuracy, exactness, minuteness, preciseness, punctuality

예 *He handled it with the preciseness of an automaton.*

---

era [íərə]   연대, 시대

图 a period marked by distinctive character or reckoned from a fixed point or event

图 age, date, epoch, period, time

예 *the beginning of a new era*

---

author [ɔːθər]   저자

图 someone who originates or causes or initiates something

图 composer, creator, originator, scribe writer

예 *He was the author of several complaints.*

---

explanation [èksplənéiʃən]   설명

图 a statement that makes something comprehensible by describing the relevant structure or operation or circumstances etc

图 definition, elucidation, explication, interpretation, meaning

예 *The explanation was very simple.*

---

lounge [làundʒ]   어슬렁어슬렁 거리다

图 be about

图 idle, laze, loiter, loll, tarry

예 *The high school students like to loiter in the Central Square*

---

gust [gʌst]   질풍

图 a strong current of air

图 blast, blow, flurry, squall, tempest

예 *The tree was bent almost double by the gust.*

rich [rít ʃ]　　　　　　　　　　　　　　　　　　　풍부한

图 having an abundant supply of desirable qualities or substances

동 abundant, fertile, moneyed, opulent, wealthy

예 *rich in ideas*

---

grip [gríp]　　　　　　　　　　　　　　　　　　　꽉 잡다

图 hold fast or firmly

동 clench, clutch, grasp, hold, seize

예 *He gripped the steering wheel.*

---

separate [sépərèit]　　　　　　　　　　　　　　　가르다

图 divide into parts or portions

동 dissever, divide, part, segregate, split

예 divide, split

---

boredom [bɔ́:rdəm]　　　　　　　　　　　　　　　지루함

图 the feeling of being bored by something tedious

동 disinterest, dullness, ennui, tedium, weariness

예 *relieve the boredom*

---

instant [ínstənt]　　　　　　　　　　　　　　　　즉시

图 occurring with no delay

동 exigent, immediate, momentary, pressing, prompt

예 *instant gratification*

---

discipline [dísəplin]　　　　　　　　　　　　　훈련받다

图 develop behavior by instruction and practice

동 chastise, punish, raise, school, train

예 *Parents must discipline their children.*

Day 1

bark [bάːrk]   짖다
- 뜻 speak in an unfriendly tone
- 동 bay, growl, howl, skin, yap
- 예 *She barked into the dictaphone.*

imprison [imprizn]   수감하다
- 뜻 lock up or confine, in or as in a jail
- 동 confine, gaol, incarcerate, jail, restrain
- 예 *The murderer was imprisoned for the rest of his life.*

despite [dispàit]   무례
- 뜻 lack of respect accompanied by a feeling of intense dislike
- 동 contempt, disdain, grudge, malice, rancor
- 예 *He was held in despite.*

peace [píːs]   평화
- 뜻 harmonious relations
- 동 calmness, pax, quietness, serenity, stillness
- 예 *The roommates lived in peace together.*

record [rikɔ́ːrd]   기록하다
- 뜻 be or provide a memorial to a person or an event
- 동 enroll, enter, note, register, write
- 예 *We recorded the Dead.*

subtle [sʌtl]   미묘한
- 뜻 difficult to detect or grasp by the mind or analyze
- 동 abstract, esoteric, incomprehensible, obscure, unfathomable
- 예 *His whole attitude had undergone a subtle change.*

primitive [prímətiv]   원시의
- 뜻 belonging to an early stage of technical development
- 동 aboriginal, original, primaeval, primeval, pristine
- 예 *primitive movies of the 1890s*

---

flush [flʌʃ]   홍조를 띠다
- 뜻 turn red, as if in embarrassment or shame
- 동 blush, crimson, pinken, redden, suffuse
- 예 *The girl flushed when a young man whistled as she walked by.*

---

cost [kɔːst]   비용
- 뜻 value measured by what must be given or done or undergone to obtain something
- 동 charge, expense, price, rate, value
- 예 *The cost in human life was enormous.*

---

hardly [háːrdli]   거의~않다
- 뜻 almost not
- 동 infrequently, rarely, scarcely, seldom, uncommonly
- 예 *He hardly ever goes fishing.*

---

landscape [lǽndskèip]   풍경
- 뜻 an expanse of scenery that can be seen in a single view
- 동 decor, scenery, spectacle, view, vista
- 예 *a desert landscape*

---

emotional [imóuʃənl]   감정적인
- 뜻 excessively affected by emotion
- 동 affective, aroused, emotive, sentimental, sensitive
- 예 *He would become emotional over nothing at all.*

---

terminate [tərməneit]   끝내다
- 圏 have an end, in a temporal, spatial, or quantitative sense
- 동 cease, conclude, end, finish, stop
- 예 *Your rights terminate where you infringe upon the rights of other.*

reach [ríːtʃ]   ~에 도달하다
- 圏 reach a destination, either real or abstract
- 동 arrive, extend, come, gain, stretch
- 예 *The water reached the doorstep.*

create [kriéit]   창조하다
- 圏 make or cause to be or to become
- 동 form, generate, make, originate, produce
- 예 *create a furor*

disaster [dizǽstər]   재앙
- 圏 a state of extreme ruin and misfortune
- 동 affliction, calamity, evil, misfortune, mishap
- 예 *His policies were a disaster.*

protect [prətékt]   보호하다
- 圏 shield from danger, injury, destruction, or damage
- 동 defend, guard, keep, preserve, shield
- 예 *Weatherbeater protects your roof from the rain.*

fortunate [fɔːrtʃənət]   행운의
- 圏 having unexpected good fortune
- 동 auspicious, favorable, lucky, prosperous, successful
- 예 *a fortunate choice*

heal [híːl]　　　　　　　　　　　　　　　　고치다

图 provide a cure for, make healthy again

图 cicatrize, cure, recover, remedy, treat

예 *The treatment healed the boy's acne.*

---

battlefield [bǽtlfiːld]　　　　　　　　　싸움터

图 a region where a battle is being (or has been) fought

图 arena, battleground, field, front, salient

예 *They made a tour of Civil War battlefields.*

---

savage [sǽvidʒ]　　　　　　　　　　　　야만스런

图 wild and menacing

图 barbaric, brutal, ferocious, truculent, wild

예 *a pack of savage dogs*

---

regular [regjulər]　　　　　통상의, 보통의, 언제나의

图 in accordance with fixed order or procedure or principle

图 normal, common, ordinary, routine, typical

예 *regular meals*

---

audience [ɔːdiəns]　　　　　　　　　　　　청중

图 a gathering of spectators or listeners at a (usually public) performance

图 assemblage, crowd, gathering, public, spectators

예 *Someone in the audience began to cough.*

---

suppose [səpóuz]　　　　　　　　가정하다, 추측하다

图 expect, believe, or suppose

图 conjecture, estimate, guess, posit, suspect

예 *I suppose she is angry at me for standing her up.*

---

private [pràivət]   사적인

图 confined to particular persons or groups or providing privacy

图 individual, intimate, particular, own, personal

예 *private discussions*

barrier [bǽriər]   장벽

图 any condition that makes it difficult to make progress or to achieve an objective

图 fence, hindrance, impediment, obstacle, obstruction

예 *Intolerance is a barrier to understanding.*

*Vocabulary/Expressions

Day 2

environment [invaiǝrǝnmǝnt]   환경

图 the totality of surrounding conditions

图 ambience, atmosphere, entourage, medium, setting

예 *He longed for the comfortable environment of his living room.*

---

stiff [stíf]   단호한

图 marked by firm determination or resolution

图 firm, steadfast, steady, unfaltering, unwavering

예 *a man of stiff perseverence*

---

bump [bʌmp]   충돌하다

图 knock against with force or violence

图 crash, hit, impinge, knock, strike

예 *My car bumped into the tree.*

---

rod [rád]   막대

图 a long thin implement made of metal or wood

图 bar, cane, stick, wand, pole

예 *a curtain rod*

---

facility [fǝsílǝti]   재주

图 skillful performance or ability without difficulty

图 ability, adeptness, adroitness, deftness, quickness

예 *He was famous for his facility as an archer.*

---

effect [ifékt]   결과

图 a phenomenon that follows and is caused by some previous phenomenon

图 consequence, impact, outcome, result, upshot

예 *The magnetic effect was greater when the rod was lengthwise.*

13

stylish [stàili∫]   맵시있는

图 having elegance or taste or refinement in manners or dress

동 chic, dressy, elegant, fashionable, modish

예 *the stylish resort of Gstadd*

---

prey [préi]   먹이

图 a person who is the aim of an attack by some hostile person or influence

동 booty, casualty, loot, quarry, victim

예 *the prey of a manhunt*

---

thrilling [θrílin]   소름끼치는

图 causing a surge of emotion or excitement;

동 breathtaking, exciting, startling, stirring, sensational

예 *She gave an thrilling performance.*

---

energetic [ènərdʒétik]   활기찬

图 possessing or exerting or displaying energy

동 active, dynamic, peppy, strenuous, vigorous

예 *an energetic group of hikers*

---

passenger [pǽsəndʒər]   승객

图 a traveler riding in a vehicle who is not operating it

동 fare, rider, traveler, traveller, voyager

예 *passenger name record*

---

nutritious [njutrí∫əs]   영양이 되는

图 of or providing nourishment

동 alimental, alimentary, nourishing, nutrient, nutritive

예 *good nutritious stew*

---

analysis [ənǽləsis]   분석
圏 an investigation of the component parts of a whole and their relations in making up the whole
동 assay, examination, evaluation, interpretation, reasoning
예 *make an analysis of*

passion [pǽʃən]   열정
圏 any object of warm affection or devotion
동 ardor, craving, desire, infatuation, lust
예 *He has a passion for cock fighting.*

charge [tʃáːrdʒ]   청구 금액, 요금
圏 the price charged for some article or service
동 price, cost, payment, expense, expenditure
예 *the admission charge*

fence [féns]   울타리
圏 a barrier that serves to enclose an area
동 barrier, enclosure, hedge, inclosure, railing
예 *a chain-link fence*

pleased [plíːzd]   좋아하는
圏 experiencing or manifesting pleasure
동 content, delighted, glad, joyful, satisfied
예 *greatly highly pleased*

concept [kánsept]   개념
圏 an abstract or general idea inferred or derived from specific instances
동 idea, intention, notion, supposition, thought
예 *formulate a concept*

measure [méʒər]   측정하다

图 determine the measurements of something or somebody, take measurements of

图 estimate, gage, mete, survey, weigh

예 *Measure the length of the wall.*

ordinarily [ɔːrdənɛ̀ərəli]   보통

图 under normal conditions

图 commonly, generally, normally, unremarkably, usually

예 *Ordinarily she was late.*

flexible [fléksəbl]   탄력적인

图 able to adjust readily to different conditions

图 elastic, limber, pliant, resilient, springy

예 *an elastic clause in a contract*

newly [njúːli]   최근에

图 very recently

图 anew, freshly, just, lately, recently

예 *They are newly married.*

undeniable [ʌndinàiəbl]   부정하기 어려운

图 not possible to deny

图 indisputable, incontestable, incontrovertible, irrefutable, unquestionable

예 *undeniable musical talent*

progressive [prəgresiv]   전진하는, 점진하는

图 favoring or promoting progress

图 advanced, gradual, growing, accelerating, escalating

예 *progressive schools*

expel [ikspel]　　　　　　　　　　　　　　　　　　　내쫓다

图 remove from a position or office

동 chase, discharge, dismiss, exile, proscribe

예 *The chairman was expeled after he misappropriated funds.*

---

reform [ri:fɔ:rm]　　　　　　　　　　　　　　　　　　개정하다

图 make changes for improvement in order to remove abuse and injustices

동 amend, improve, mend, reclaim, regenerate

예 *reform a political system*

---

optimistic [àptəmístik]　　　　　　　　　　　　　　　낙천적인

图 expecting the best in this best of all possible worlds

동 affirmative, hopeful, positive, sanguine, upbeat

예 *optimistic plans*

---

quarrel [kwɔ:rəl]　　　　　　　　　　　　　　　　　말다툼하다

图 have a disagreement over something

동 altercate, argue, brawl, dispute, wrangle

예 *These two fellows are always quarreling over something.*

---

limitation [lìmətéiʃən]　　　　　　　　　　　　　　　　제한

图 the greatest amount of something that is possible or allowed

동 confinement, qualification, restraint, restriction, stint

예 *There are limitations on the amount you can bet.*

---

employee [implɔii:]　　　　　　　　　　　　　　　　　고용인

图 a worker who is hired to perform a job

동 clerk, personnel, servant, staff, worker

예 *make an employee redundant*

---

ripen [ràipən]   익다

医 cause to ripen or develop fully

동 cultivate, maturate, mature, mellow, season

예 *The sun ripens the fruit.*

---

vivid [vívid]   생생한

医 evoking lifelike images within the mind

동 alive, lively, graphic, picturesque, vivacious

예 *a vivid description*

---

order [ɔ́ːrdər]   명령

医 a command given by a superior that must be obeyed

동 behest, commandment, decree, injunction, ukase

예 *The British ships dropped anchor and waited for orders from London.*

---

remain [riméin]   남다

医 continue in a place, position, or situation

동 abide, keep, last, rest, stay

예 *After graduation, she remained on in Cambridge as a student adviser.*

---

tempt [témpt]   유혹하다

医 induce into action by using one's charm

동 allure, entice, inveigle, lure, seduce

예 *She charmed him into giving her all his money.*

---

hateful [héitfəl]   미운

医 characterized by malice

동 abhorrent, detestable, heinous, loathsome, obnoxious

예 *a hateful thing to do*

---

compose [kəmpouz]   구성하다

图 form the substance of

图 be made of, comprise, constitute, construct, form

예 *Greed and ambition composed his personality.*

---

gap [gǽp]   갈라진 틈

图 an open or empty space in or between things

图 aperture, crack, hole, opening, space

예 *There was a small gap between the trees.*

---

dissatisfaction [dìssætisfǽk ʃ ən]   불만

图 the feeling of being displeased and discontent

图 complaint, disaffection, discontent, displeasure, unhappiness

예 *He was never slow to express his dissatisfaction with the service he received.*

---

conservation [kànsərvei ʃ ən]   보존, 유지

图 an occurrence   of improvement by virtue of preventing loss or injury or other change

图 preservation, keeping, conservancy, maintenance, protection

예 *conservation area*

---

apparently [əpǽrəntli]   외관상으로는

图 from appearances alone

图 ostensibly, outwardly, plausibly, seemingly, superficially

예 *The child is apparently healthy but the doctor is concerned.*

---

head [hed]   나아가다

图 to go or travel towards

图 advance, conduct, direct, lead, proceed

예 *We were headed for the mountains.*

---

aware [əwέər]   알아차리고

圐 having or showing knowledge or understanding or realization or perception

동 aware, cognisant, conscious, informed, sensible

예 *became aware of her surroundings*

---

unique [juːniːk]   유일한, 독특한

圐 radically distinctive and without equal

동 only, rare, solitary, uncommon, particular

예 *Bach was unique in his handling of counterpoint*

---

offend [əfend]   성나게 하다

圐 cause to feel resentment or indignation

동 pique, displease, irritate, annoy, disgruntle

예 *Her tactless remark offended me.*

---

ground [gràund]   지면

圐 the solid part of the earth's surface

동 earth, field, floor, land, soil

예 *He dropped the logs on the ground.*

---

fertilize [fɛrtəlàiz]   비옥하게하다

圐 provide with fertilizers or add nutrients to

동 enrich, fecundate, impregnate, inseminate, manure

예 *We should fertilize soil if we want to grow healthy plants.*

---

successive [səksésiv]   연속하는

圐 in regular succession without gaps

동 consecutive, ensuing, following, sequential, serial

예 *successive concerts*

---

headquarters [hedkwɔːrtərz]   본부

図 the office that serves as the administrative center of an enterprise

뜻 central office, head office, home base, home office, main office

예 *Many companies have their headquarters in New York.*

comfort [kʌmfərt]   위로하다

図 give moral or emotional strength to

뜻 alleviate, console, solace, soothe, relieve

예 *comfort each other*

*Vocabulary/Expressions

Day 3

---

condition [kəndiʃən]   상태

医 a state at a particular time

图 state, situation, circumstance, fettle, position

예 *a condition of disrepair*

---

precise [prisais]   정확한

医 sharply exact or accurate or delimited

图 accurate, definite, exact, scrupulous, strict

예 *arrived at the precise moment*

---

situation [sìtʃuéiʃən]   상태

医 the general state of things

图 circumstance, condition, fettle, state, position

예 *The present international situation is dangerous.*

---

basis [béisis]   기초

医 the fundamental assumptions from which something is begun or developed or calculated or explained

图 base, cornerstone, groundwork, foundation, fundament

예 *The whole argument rested on a basis of conjecture.*

---

insistent [insistənt]   끈질긴

医 repetitive and persistent

图 dogged, importunate, persistent, pertinacious, tenacious

예 *the bluejay's insistent cry*

---

obviously [ábviəsli]   명백하게

医 readily perceived by the eye or the intellect

图 apparently, clearly, evidently, manifestly, plainly

예 *The answer is obviously wrong.*

---

distinct [distíŋkt]
뚜렷한
- 图 clearly or sharply defined to the mind
- 图 clear, definite, distinguishable, obvious, perspicuous
- 예 *distinct evidence of tampering*

encounter [inkáuntər]
만나다
- 图 come together
- 图 brush, face, meet, rendezvous, see
- 예 *I'll probably encounter you at the meeting.*

scatter [skǽtər]
흩뿌리다
- 图 move away from each other
- 图 disperse, dissipate, spread out, strew, dissipate
- 예 *The children scattered in all directions when the teacher approached.*

appearance [əpíərəns]
외관
- 图 outward or visible aspect of a person or thing
- 图 aspect, face, look, presence, semblance, shape
- 예 *I tried to describe his appearance to the police.*

criticize [krítəsàiz]
비판하다
- 图 find fault with
- 图 animadvert, censure, reprimand, review, scrutinize
- 예 *The paper criticized the new movie.*

use [jú:z]
사용하다
- 图 take or consume regularly or habitually
- 图 capitalize, handle, manage, operate, utilize
- 예 *She uses drugs rarely.*

graceful [gréisfəl]   우아한

图 suggesting taste, ease, and wealth

图 charming, elegant, exquisite, refined, tasteful

예 *her graceful movements*

---

annoy [ənɔ́i]   성가시게 굴다

图 disturb, especially by minor irritations

图 bother, disturb, irritate, pester, vex

예 *annoy greatly*

---

raw [rɔ:]   가공하지 않은

图 being unprocessed or manufactured using only simple or minimal processes

图 crude, green, natural, rough, unworked

예 *raw wool*

---

minor [màinər]   중요치않은

图 of lesser importance or stature or rank

图 lesser, junior, petty, secondary, small

예 *a minor poet*

---

emotion [imóuʃən]   감동

图 any strong feeling

图 agitation, excitement, feeling, sentiment, sensation

예 *charged with emotion*

---

surveillance [sərvéiləns]   감시

图 close observation of a person or group (usually by the police)

图 control, inspection, observation, oversight, supervision

예 *surveillance camera*

inefficient [inifíʃ ənt]　　　　　　무능한

- 圐 lacking the ability or skill to perform effectively
- 圐 incapable, incompetent, ineffective, inefficacious, unable
- 圀 *inefficient workers*

additional [ədíʃ ənl]　　　　　　부가적인

- 圐 further or added
- 圐 accessory, extra, further, subsidiary, supplementary
- 圀 *an additional pair of shoes*

insurance [inʃ uərəns]　　　　　　보험

- 圐 written contract or certificate of insurance
- 圐 assurance, coverage, guarantee, indemnity, safeguard
- 圀 *You should have read the small print on your insurance.*

burden [bɚdn]　　　　　　짐을 지우다

- 圐 impose a task upon, assign a responsibility to
- 圐 charge, load, saddle, tax, weight
- 圀 *He burdend her with cleaning up all the files over the weekend.*

merely [míərli]　　　　　　단지

- 圐 and nothing more
- 圐 but, just, only, purely, simply
- 圀 *I was merely asking.*

companion [kəmpǽnjən]　　　　　　동료

- 圐 a friend who is frequently in the company of another
- 圐 associate, comrade, confrere, fellow, mate
- 圀 *drinking companions*

Day 3

prospect [práspekt]   전망
- 뜻 the possibility of future success
- 동 expectancy, outlook, perspective, view, vista
- 예 *His prospects as a writer are excellent.*

influence [ínfluəns]   영향을 끼치다
- 뜻 have and exert influence or effect
- 동 affect, impel, operate, sway, work
- 예 *The artist's work influenced the young painter.*

prevent [privént]   막다
- 뜻 keep from happening or arising
- 동 avert, hinder, inhibit, obstruct, prohibit
- 예 *prevent crime*

pose [póuz]   자세
- 뜻 a posture assumed by models for photographic or artistic purposes
- 동 attitude, condition, position, posture, stance
- 예 *strike a pose*

bumpy [bʌmpi]   울퉁불퉁한
- 뜻 causing or characterized by jolts and irregular movements
- 동 jolty, jumpy, rough, rugged, uneven
- 예 *a bumpy ride*

endless [éndlis]   끝이 없는
- 뜻 tiresomely long
- 동 eternal, infinite, interminable, perpetual, unending
- 예 *endless debates*

Day 3

enter [éntər] ~에 들어가다

뜻 to come or go into

동 access, infiltrate, insert, invade, penetrate

예 *The boat entered an area of shallow marshes.*

---

erase [iréis] 지우다

뜻 remove from memory or existence

동 efface, expunge, delete, obliterate, rub

예 *The Turks erased the Armenians in 1915.*

---

quality [kwáləti] 품질

뜻 a degree or grade of excellence or worth

동 attribute, class, grade, merit, property

예 *The quality of students has risen.*

---

incorrect [ìnkərékt] 부정확한

뜻 not in conformity with fact or truth

동 erroneous, faulty, inaccurate, mistaken, wrong

예 *The report in the paper is incorrect.*

---

solemn [sáləm] 엄숙한

뜻 characterized by a firm and humorless belief in the validity of your opinions

동 austere, earnest, portentous, sincere, weighty

예 *Both sides were deeply in solemn, even passionate.*

---

barbarism [bá:rbərìzm] 야만성

뜻 a brutal barbarous savage act

동 atrocity, barbarity, brutality, savagery, uncivilizedness

예 *outright barbarism*

---

accumulate [əkjúːmjulèit]   모으다

图 collect or gather

图 amass, assemble, collect, heap, gather

예 *Journals are accumulating in my office.*

---

adversity [ædvɛrsəti]   불운

图 a state of misfortune or affliction

图 distress, hardship, misfortune, suffering, torment

예 *a life of adversity*

---

trustworthy [trʌstwɛrði]   믿을 수 있는

图 worthy of trust or belief

图 certain, dependable, reliable, responsible, safe

예 *a trustworthy report*

---

constitute [kánstətjuːt]   구성하다

图 form or compose

图 compose, comprise, establish, form, institute

예 *These constitute my entire belonging.*

---

resolve [rizálv]   결정하다

图 bring to an end

图 adjudicate, decide, determine, intend, settle

예 *The judge resolved the case in favor of the plaintiff.*

---

resist [rizíst]   ~에 저항하다

图 withstand the force of something

图 abide, fend, oppose, stand, withstand

예 *The mountain climbers had to resist against the ice and snow.*

---

rigid [ridʒid]   단단한

- 图 incapable of or resistant to bending
- 图 firm, hard, inflexible, stiff, unbending
- 예 *a rigid strip of metal*

diminish [dimíniʃ]   줄이다

- 图 decrease in size, extent, or range
- 图 abate, decrease, fall, lessen, reduce
- 예 *The amount of homework diminished towards the end of the semester.*

reputation [repjuteiʃən]   평판

- 图 the general estimation that the public has for a person
- 图 celebrity, fame, renown, report, repute
- 예 *He was a person of bad reputation.*

leap [líːp]   껑충뛰다

- 图 move forward by leaps and bounds
- 图 bounce, hop, jump, spring, vault
- 예 *The child leapt across the puddle.*

finite [fàinait]   한정된

- 图 bounded or limited in magnitude or spatial or temporal extent
- 图 confined, limited, narrow, qualified, restricted
- 예 *finite resources*

cliff [klíf]   낭떠러지

- 图 a steep high face of rock
- 图 crag, escarpment, precipice, rock, wall
- 예 *He stood on a high cliff overlooking the town.*

Day 3

tolerate [tɑ́lərèit]   관대하게 다루다

- 图 allow the presence of or allow without opposing or prohibiting
- 图 allow, bear, endure, permit, stand
- 예 *We cannot tolerate smoking in the hospital.*

diffusion [difjúːʒən]   발산

- 图 the act of dispersing or diffusing something
- 图 dispersion, dissemination, propagation, scattering, spreading
- 예 *the diffusion of knowledge*

*Vocabulary/Expressions

refer [rifɜr]   관련되다
图 be relevant to
图 apply, concern, pertain, relate, touch
예 *There were lots of questions referring to her talk.*

adequate [ǽdikwət]   충분한
图 sufficient for the purpose
图 appropriate, enough, fit, sufficient, suitable
예 *an adequate income*

exclusion [iksklú:ʒən]   제외
图 the act of forcing out someone or something
图 elimination, exception, expulsion, preclusion, riddance
예 *the child's exclusion from school*

balance [bǽləns]   균형
图 a state of equilibrium
图 equilibrium, equipoise, equivalence, poise, symmetry
예 *throw a person off his balance*

stuff [stʌf]   물건, 사물
图 the tangible substance that goes into the makeup of a physical object
图 material, substance, matter
예 *wheat is the stuff they use to make bread*

celebrate [seləbreit]   축하하다
图 have a celebration
图 commemorate, extol, glorify, praise, solemnize
예 *After the exam, the students were celebrating.*

perhaps [pərhǽps]   아마, 어쩌면

뜻 by chance

동 maybe, peradventure, perchance, possibly, probably

예 *Perhaps she will call tomorrow.*

---

elect [ilékt]   선거하다

뜻 select by a vote for an office or membership

동 choose, opt, pick, select, vote

예 *We elected him chairman of the board.*

---

temperature [témpərətʃər]   온도

뜻 the degree of hotness or coldness of a body or environment

동 degrees, fever, heat, incalescence, pyrexia

예 *take a person's temperature*

---

handle [hǽndl]   다루다

뜻 interact in a certain way

동 care, deal, operate, manipulate, treat

예 *Treat him with caution, please.*

---

vague [veig]   막연한

뜻 not clearly understood or expressed

동 ambiguous, equivocal, indistinct, obscure, tenebrous

예 *an vague turn of phrase*

---

shout [ʃàut]   외치다

뜻 utter in a loud voice

동 bawl, exclaim, roar, scream, whoop

예 *My grandmother is hard of hearing--you'll have to shout.*

---

contrast [kántræst]   대조하다

图 to show differences when compared

동 collate, compare, differentiate, distinguish, oppose

예 *The students contrast considerably in their artistic abilities.*

---

nighttime [nàittàim]   밤

图 the time after sunset and before sunrise while it is dark outside

동 bedtime, dusk, evening, night, nightfall

예 *nighttime staff*

---

informed [infɔ:rmd]   교양있는

图 having much knowledge or education

동 aware, cognizant, conversant, learned, knowing

예 *an informed public*

---

frustration [frʌstréiʃən]   좌절

图 the feeling that accompanies an experience of being thwarted in attaining
your goals

동 defeat, disappointment, dissatisfaction, hindrance, unfulfillment

예 *express one's frustration*

---

mobile [móubəl, -bi:l]   이동할 수 있는

图 moving or capable of moving readily

동 movable, moving, moveable, portable, travelling

예 *a mobile missile system*

---

inhabit [inhǽbit]   살다

图 inhabit or live in

동 abide, dwell, live, populate, reside

예 *The people inhabited the islands that are now deserted.*

extra [ekstrə]   여분의

图 more than is needed, desired, or required

통 excess, redundant, superfluous, supernumerary, surplus

예 *found some extra change lying on the dresser*

---

fitness [fítnis]   적합

图 the quality of being suitable

통 aptitude, aptness, pertinence, propriety, suitability

예 *They had to prove their fitness for the position.*

---

alarm [əlá:rm]   놀라게하다

图 cause to be unpleasantly surprised

통 alarm, dismay, frighten, horrify, scare

예 *The news of the executions alarmed us.*

---

inspiration [ìnspəréiʃən]   영감

图 a product of your creative thinking and work

통 afflatus, creativity, illumination, motivation, stimulus

예 *He had little respect for the inspirations of other artists.*

---

concerned [kənsɝnd]   걱정스러운

图 feeling or showing worry or solicitude

통 anxious, attentive, solicitous, uneasy, worried

예 *concerned parents of youthful offenders*

---

persistence [pərsístəns]   영속

图 continuing or repeating behavior

통 endurance, perseveration, perseverance, stubbornness, tenacity

예 *His persistence continued to the point where it was no longer appropriate.*

---

comfort [kʌmfərt]   위로하다

- 뜻 give moral or emotional strength to
- 동 alleviate, console, solace, soothe, relieve
- 예 *comfort each other.*

freight [freit]   화물

- 뜻 goods carried by a large vehicle
- 동 cargo, lading, load, shipment, consignment
- 예 *freight car*

entirely [intàiərli]   완전히

- 뜻 to a complete degree or to the full or entire extent
- 동 altogether, completely, perfectly, totally, wholly
- 예 *It was entirely different from what we expected.*

accentuate [æksént ʃ uèit]   강조하다

- 뜻 to stress, single out as important
- 동 accent, emphasize, punctuate, stress, underline
- 예 *In Farsi, you accentuate the last syllable of each word.*

store [stɔːr]   공급해두다

- 뜻 keep or lay aside for future use
- 동 accumulate, deposit, put, save, stockpile
- 예 *Store grain for the winter.*

race [réis]   경쟁하다

- 뜻 compete in a race
- 동 compete, contest, run, scramble, sprint
- 예 *Let's race and see who gets there first.*

odd [ád]   이상한

뜻 beyond or deviating from the usual or expected

동 eccentric, peculiar, quaint, strange, weird

예 *the odd aromatic odor of cloves*

---

supply [səplái]   공급하다

뜻 give something useful or necessary to

동 provide, render, furnish, grant, purvey

예 *We supplied the room with an electrical heater.*

---

suffer [sʌfər]   견디다

뜻 put up with something or somebody unpleasant

동 bear, digest, endure, stand, tolerate

예 *The new secretary had to suffer a lot of unprofessional remarks.*

---

atmosphere [ǽtməsfìər]   분위기

뜻 a distinctive but intangible quality surrounding a person or thing

동 air, ambience, aura, environment, entourage

예 *The house had a neglected atmosphere.*

---

valuable [vǽljuəbl]   값진

뜻 having great material or monetary value especially for use or exchange

동 costly, precious, rich, valued, worthy

예 *a valuable diamond*

---

loneliness [lóunlinis]   고독, 외로움

뜻 sadness resulting from being forsaken or abandoned

동 desolation, isolation, lonesomeness, solitariness, solitude

예 *complete utter loneliness*

---

disappointed [dìsəpɔ́intid]

실망한

圐 disappointingly unsuccessful

동 complaining, despondent, frustrated, saddened, unsatisfied

몌 *disappointed expectations and thwarted ambitions*

---

consciously [kάnʃəsli]

의식하여

圐 with awareness

동 deliberately, knowingly, purposely, thoughtfully, wittingly

몌 *She consciously played with the idea of inviting them.*

---

anticipate [æntisəpeit]

예상하다

圐 regard something as probable or likely

동 expect, forebode, foresee, predict, previse

몌 *The meteorologists are expecting rain for tomorrow.*

---

continue [kəntínjuː]

계속하다

圐 keep or maintain in unaltered condition

동 endure, last, preserve, proceed, uphold

몌 *continue the family tradition*

---

retouch [rìːtʌ́tʃ]

수정하다

圐 alter so as to produce a more desirable appearance

동 amend, correct, improve, modify, revise

몌 *This photograph has been retouched.*

---

stand [stǽnd]

견디다

圐 put up with something or somebody unpleasant

동 abide, bear, endure, stay, stop

몌 *I cannot stand his constant criticism.*

---

elevation [eləvei ʃ ən]   고도

国 the highest level or degree attainable

国 altitude, eminence, height, roof, top

예 *at the elevation of her career*

---

ransportation [trænspərtéi ʃ ən]   수송

国 the act of moving something from one location to another

国 carrying, conveyance, portage, traffic, transport

예 *means of transportation*

---

avoid [əvɔid]   피하다

国 prevent the occurrence of

国 dodge, elude, eschew, evade, shun

예 *Let's avoid a confrontation.*

---

popular [pápjulər]   인기있는

国 regarded with great favor, approval, or affection especially by the general
   public

国 celebrated, famous, favorite, notorious, well-known

예 *a popular tourist attraction*

---

criterion [kraitíəriən]   표준, 기준

国 a basis for comparison

国 measure, norm, standard, touchstone, yardstick

예 *The schools comply with federal criterions.*

---

consciousness [kán ʃ əsnis]   의식

国 having knowledge of

国 awareness, conscience, mind, knowledge, sense

예 *He had no consciousness of his mistakes.*

---

congratulation [kəngræt ʃ uléi ʃ ən]　　　　축하

图 an expression of pleasure at the success or good fortune of another

동 adulation, compliment, felicitation, greeting, salute

예 *I sent them my sincere congratulations on their marriage.*

---

instrument [instrəmənt]　　　　기계, 기구, 도구

图 a device that requires skill for proper use

동 tool, implement, equipment, machine, appliance

예 *drawing instrument*

---

*Vocabulary/Expressions

dealer [díːlər]   상인
- 图 someone who purchases and maintains an inventory of goods to be sold
- 图 merchant, monger, seller, tradesman, trafficker
- 예 *a reputable dealer*

---

acquisition [ækwəzi∫ən]   획득
- 图 the act of contracting or assuming or acquiring possession of something
- 图 acquirement, attainment, gain, procurement, purchase
- 예 *the acquisition of wealth*

---

trick [trík]   트릭, 속임수
- 图 a cunning or deceitful action or device
- 图 artifice, gimmick, prank, ruse, wile
- 예 *He played a trick on me.*

---

shortage [∫ɔːrtidʒ]   부족, 결핍
- 图 the property of being an amount by which something is less than expected or required
- 图 dearth, deficiency, insufficiency, lack, scarcity
- 예 *an acute desperate shortage*

---

swift [swíft]   빠른
- 图 moving very fast
- 图 expeditious, fast, prompt, rapid, speedy
- 예 *a swift current*

---

commoner [kámənər]   평민, 대중
- 图 a person who holds no title
- 图 bourgeois, bourgeoisie, citizen, peasant, plebeian
- 예 *a powerless commoner*

40

adversity [ædvɛ́rsəti]   불운

图 a state of misfortune or affliction

图 distress, hardship, misfortune, suffering, torment

예 *a life of adversity*

attitude [ǽtitjùːd]   태도, 자세

图 the arrangement of the body and its limbs

图 bearing, manner, position, posture, stance

예 *He assumed an attitude of surrender.*

shiny [ʃàini]   빛나는

图 reflecting light

图 brilliant, glossy, lustrous, polished, shining

예 *shining white enamel*

religious [rilídʒəs]   종교의

图 concerned with sacred matters or religion or the church

图 devout, godly, pious, sacred, spiritual

예 *religious texts*

cry [krài]   부르짖다

图 utter a sudden loud cry

图 bawl, call, scream, shout, wail

예 *She cried with pain when the doctor inserted the needle.*

satisfying [sǽtisfàiiŋ]   만족을 주는

图 providing freedom from worry

图 delightful, favorable, fulfilling, gratifying, rewarding

예 *emotionally satisfying*

separation [sepərei ʃ ən]　　　　　　　　분리, 분할
囷 coming apart
圐 detachment, segregation, divorce, division, partition
몡 *the separation of wheat from chaff*

transmit [trænsmít]　　　　　　　　　부치다
囷 transfer to another
圐 carry, communicate, convey, send, transfer
몡 *transmit a disease*

evolve [iválv]　　　　　　　　　서서히 발전하다
囷 gain through experience
圐 acquire, develop, obtain, progress, unfold
몡 *Children must evolve a sense of right and wrong.*

renew [rinju:]　　　　　　　　　새롭게 하다
囷 reestablish on a new, usually improved, basis or make new or like new
圐 regenerate, refurbish, renovate, freshen, recreate
몡 *They renewed their membership*

connection [kənek ʃ ən]　　　　　　　관계, 관련
囷 a relation between things or event
圐 contact, association, reciporcity
몡 *There was a connection between eating that pickle and having that nightmare.*

regardless [rigá:rdlis]　　　　　　부주의한, 관심없는
囷 without due thought or consideration
圐 careless, indifferent, unconcerned, inattentive, heedless
몡 *crushing the blooms with regardless tread*

isolate [àisəlèit] 고립시키다

图 place or set apart

통 detach, insulate, seclude, segregate, withdraw

예 *They isolated the political prisoners from the other inmates.*

command [kəmǽnd] 명령하다

图 make someone do something

통 bid, direct, dominate, enjoin, order

예 *The author commands a fair hearing from his readers.*

compile [kəmpail] 수집하다

图 get or gather together

통 accumulate, amass, collect, congregate, muster

예 *She compiled a small fortune.*

secret [síːkrit] 비밀의

图 conducted with or marked by hidden aims or methods

통 clandestine, furtive, hidden, privy, undercover

예 *secret missions*

spectacular [spektǽkjulər] 장관의

图 having a quality that thrusts itself into attention

통 impressive, outstanding, prominent, salient, striking

예 *a spectacular rise in prices*

activity [æktivəti] 활동

图 any specific activity

통 action, exertion, movement, operation, work

예 *They avoided all recreational activity.*

valid [vǽlid]   근거가 확실한, 정확한, 정당한

뜻 well grounded in logic or truth or having legal force

동 convincing, accurate, credible, proven, trustworthy

예 *a valid inference*

---

disappointment [dìsəpɔ́intmənt]   실망

뜻 a feeling of dissatisfaction that results when your expectations are not realized

동 anticlimax, chagrin, displeasure, frustration, unfulfillment

예 *His hopes were so high he was doomed to disappointment.*

---

disassemble [disəsémbl]   분해하다

뜻 take apart into its constituent pieces

동 demount, dismantle, divide, separate, sever

예 *disassemble a machine*

---

naturally [nǽtʃərəli]   당연히

뜻 as might be expected

동 certainly, generally, ordinarily, surely, uniformly

예 *Naturally, the lawyer sent us a huge bill.*

---

promotion [prəmóuʃən]   촉진, 장려

뜻 the advancement of some enterprise

동 advancement, forwarding, furtherance, preferment, rise

예 *His experience in marketing resulted in the forwarding of his career.*

---

solution [səluːʃən]   해결

뜻 a statement that solves a problem or explains how to solve the problem

동 answer, explanation, explication, solving, unravelment

예 *They were trying to find a peaceful solution.*

undoubtedly [ʌndàutidli]   의심할 여지없이

图 without doubt

图 certainly, definitely, doubtless, surely, truly

몌 *It's undoubtedly very beautiful.*

---

essential [isénʃəl]   본질적인

图 absolutely necessary

图 basic, fundamental, indispensable, substantial, vital

몌 *essential tools and materials*

---

cherish [tʃériʃ]   소중히 하다

图 be fond of

图 adore, commend, esteem, glorify, respect

몌 *cherish a friendship*

---

tumble [tʌmbl]   넘어지다

图 fall down, as if collapsing

图 descend, fall, slump, topple, toss

몌 *The tower of the World Trade Center tumbled after the plane hit it.*

---

participate [pɑːrtísəpèit]   참여하다

图 be involved in

图 enter, engage, join, partake, share

몌 *participate a drug treatment program*

---

period [píəriəd]   기간

图 an amount of time

图 age, epoch, era, term, season

몌 *a time period of 30 years*

---

pedestrian [pədestriən]   보행자, 도보여행자

뜻 a person who travels by foot

동 walker, footer, hiker, jaywalker, passerby

예 *pedestrian crossing*

---

diffuse [difjú:z]   흐트러뜨리다

뜻 spread or diffuse through

동 disperse, distribute, scatter, spread, propagate

예 *diffuse every inch of the country*

---

neatly [ní:tli]   깔끔하게, 말쑥하게

뜻 with clean or organized

동 beautifully, cleanly, nicely, tastefully, trimly

예 *She put the slippers under the bed neatly.*

---

vibration [vaibréiʃən]   진동

뜻 a shaky motion

동 oscillation, quiver, shaking, trembling, tremor

예 *The vibration of his fingers as he lit his pipe.*

---

industrious [indʌstriəs]   근면한

뜻 characterized by hard work and perseverance

동 assiduous, diligent, hardworking, laborious, sedulous

예 *honest and industrious man*

---

firm [fɛrm]   확고한

뜻 marked by firm determination or resolution

동 fixed, hard, immovable, resolute, steadfast

예 *firm convictions*

---

calm [káːm]   고요한

图 not agitated

图 peaceful, serene, silent, tranquil, unagitated,

예 *spoke in a calm voice*

---

available [əvéiləbl]   이용할 수 있는

图 obtainable or accessible and ready for use or service

图 accessible, applicable, disposable, obtainable, serviceable

예 *available in many colors*

---

sadness [sǽdnis]   슬픔, 비애

图 the state of being sad

图 affliction, distress, grief, melancholy, sorrow

예 *She tired of his perpetual sadness.*

---

recent [ríːsnt]   최근의

图 of the immediate past or just previous to the present time

图 fresh, late, latter, modern, new

예 *recent buds on the apple trees*

---

profession [prəféʃən]   직업

图 the body of people in a learned occupation

图 career, metier, occupation, trade, vocation

예 *The news spread rapidly through the medical profession.*

---

grant [grǽnt]   주다

图 give as judged due or on the basis of merit

图 award, bestow, concede, confer, give

예 *The referee granted a free kick to the team.*

---

crucial [kru: ʃ əl]   중대한

图 of the greatest importance

통 critical, deciding, decisive, important, vital

예 *crucial information*

---

reveal [rivi:l]   드러내다

图 make known to the public information that was previously known only to a few people or that was meant to be kept a secret

통 disclose, divulge, expose, uncover, unwrap

예 *The actress won't reveal how old she is.*

*Vocabulary/Expressions

Day 6

reduce [ridʒúːs] 줄이다
- 图 cut down on
- 图 abate, decrease, diminish, lessen, lower
- 예 *Reduce your daily fat intake.*

ultimate [ʌ́ltəmət] 최종의, 궁극의
- 图 furthest or highest in degree or order
- 图 conclusive, final, last, terminal, uttermost
- 예 *the ultimate achievement*

intent [intént] 지향, 목적
- 图 an anticipated outcome that is intended or that guides your planned actions
- 图 aim, goal, notion, object, purpose
- 예 *His intent was to provide a new translation.*

promote [prəmout] 증진하다
- 图 contribute to the progress or growth of
- 图 advance, boost, encourage, further, raise
- 예 *I am promoting the use of computers in the classroom.*

sink [síŋk] 가라앉다
- 图 fall or descend to a lower place or level
- 图 dip, drop, fall, submerge, subside
- 예 *He sank to his knees.*

ask [ǽsk] 묻다
- 图 inquire about
- 图 demand, enquire, inquire, question, require
- 예 *I asked about their special today.*

49

obstacle [ábstəkl] 　　　　　　　　　　　　　　　　　장애

图 something immaterial that stands in the way and must be circumvented or surmounted

图 barrier, encumbrance, impediment, hindrance, obstruction

例 *Lack of imagination is an obstacle to one's advancement.*

brief [bri:f] 　　　　　　　　　　　　　　　　　　　　간결한

图 concise and succinct

图 compendious, concise, short, succinct, terse

例 *covered the matter in a brief statement*

empty [empti] 　　　　　　　　　　　　　　　　　　　　빈

图 holding or containing nothing

图 blank, void, vacant, hollow, inane

例 *an empty glass*

comprehension [kámprihén ∫ən] 　　　　　　　　　이해

图 an ability to understand the meaning or importance of something

图 apprehension, grasp, perception, realization, understanding

例 *How you can do that is beyond my comprehension.*

avenge [əvéndʒ] 　　　　　　　　　　　　　　　　　복수하다

图 take revenge for a perceived wrong

图 chastise, punish, retaliate, revenge, vindicate

例 *He wants to avenge the murder of his brother.*

absorb [æbsɔ́:rb] 　　　　　　　　　　　　　　　　　흡수하다

图 take in, also metaphorically

图 consume, devour, imbibe, ingest, soak

例 *The sponge absorbs water well.*

impression [impréʃən]　　　　　　　　　　인상, 감명

图 a clear and telling mental image

동 apprehension, memory, perception, recollection, thought

예 *The events left a permanent impression in his mind.*

---

container [kəntéinər]　　　　　　　　　　그릇, 용기

图 any object that can be used to hold things

동 case, holder, receptacle, tank, vessel

예 *Please store jam in an airtight container.*

---

error [érər]　　　　　　　　　　　　　　잘못, 실수

图 a wrong action attributable to bad judgment or ignorance or inattention

동 absurdity, fallacy, fault, mistake, wrong

예 *She was quick to point out my errors.*

---

investment [invéstmənt]　　　　　　　　　투자

图 laying out money or capital in an enterprise with the expectation of profit

동 asset, expenditure, finance, investing, venture

예 *overseas investments*

---

refuse [rifjúːz]　　　　　　　　　　　　거절하다

图 show unwillingness towards

동 cease, decline, rebuff, refrain, reject

예 *He declined to join the group on a hike.*

---

loan [loun]　　　　　　　　　　　　　　대부

图 the temporary provision of money

동 advance, accommodation, borrowing, debt, mortgage

예 *bank loan*

Day 6

envy [énvi]   부러워하다

뜻 admire enviously

동 begrudge, crave, desire, want, yearn

예 *I feel no envy at your success.*

---

equipment [ikwípmənt]   장비, 비품

뜻 an instrumentality needed for an undertaking or to perform a service

동 apparatus, devices, gear, kit, tackle

예 *audiovisual equipment*

---

sorrow [sάrou]   슬픔

뜻 sadness associated with some wrong done or some disappointment

동 dolor, grief, mourning, sadness, woe

예 *He wrote a note expressing his sorrow.*

---

lessen [lésn]   적게 하다

뜻 decrease in size, extent, or range

동 abate, belittle, decrease, diminish, reduce

예 *The cabin pressure lessen dramatically.*

---

national [nǽʃənl]   국가의, 국가적인

뜻 of or relating to or belonging to a nation or country

동 domestic, native, ethnic, public, civil

예 *national hero*

---

ranch [rǽntʃ]   대농장

뜻 farm consisting of a large tract of land along with facilities needed to raise livestock

동 estate, farm, farmstead, hacienda, plantation

예 *a chicken ranch*

standard [stǽndərd]　　　　　　　　　　　　표준, 기준

뜻 a basis for comparison

동 criterion, guideline, measure, norm, touchstone

예 *The schools comply with federal standards.*

consider [kənsidər]　　　　　　　　　　　　숙고하다

뜻 think about carefully

동 debate, deliberate, meditate, moot, ponder

예 *They considered the possibility of a strike.*

overestimate [ouvərestəmeit]　　　　　　과대평가하다

뜻 make too high an estimate of

동 amplify, magnify, overprize, overrate, overvalue

예 *He overestimated his own powers.*

bang [bǽŋ]　　　　　　　　　　　　　　　탕 치다

뜻 strike violently

동 beat, hit, knock, slam, strike

예 *Bang the ball.*

think [θíŋk]　　　　　　　　　　　　　　생각하다

뜻 judge or regard

동 believe, conceive, consider, guess, suppose

예 *I think her to be very smart.*

nap [nǽp]　　　　　　　　　　　　　　　잠깐 졸다

뜻 take a siesta

동 catnap, drowse, sleep, snooze, siesta

예 *She naps everyday after lunch for an hour.*

gesture [dʒéstʃər]　　　　　　　　몸짓을 하다

뜻 show, express or direct through movement

동 gesticulate, indicate, motion, signalize, wave

예 *He gestured his desire to leave.*

range [reindʒ]　　　　　　　　정렬시키다

뜻 lay out orderly or logically in a line or as if in a line

동 align, categorize, classify, line, order

예 *range the clothes*

temper [témpər]　　　　　　　　기질, 성질

뜻 a characteristic habitual or relatively temporary state of feeling

동 character, disposition, humor, mood, nature

예 *He was in a bad temper.*

impulsive [impʌlsiv]　　　　　　　　충동적인

뜻 determined by chance or impulse or whim rather than by necessity or reason

동 abrupt, extemporaneous, impetuous, sudden, unpremeditated

예 *a impulsive refusal*

indirect [indərékt]　　　　　　　　똑바르지 않은, 우회하는

뜻 having intervening factors or persons or influences

동 circuitous, collateral, devious, oblique, roundabout

예 *reflection from the ceiling provided a soft indirect light*

entire [intaiər]　　　　　　　　전체의

뜻 constituting the full quantity or extent

동 all, general, thorough, total, whole

예 *An entire town devastated by an earthquake.*

alter [ɔ́:ltər]   변경하다

图 cause to change

图 change, convert, modify, shift, transform

예 *The discussion has altered my thinking about the issue.*

---

disharmony [dìshá:rməni]   불일치, 부조화

图 a lack of harmony

图 disaccord, discordance, friction, inharmoniousness, strife

예 *religious disharmony*

---

element [éləmənt]   요소, 성분

图 an abstract part of something

图 component, constituent, factor, ingredient, section

예 *Jealousy was a element of his character.*

---

worship [wɛ́rʃip]   숭배하다, 존경하다

图 show devotion to a deity

图 adore, deify, idolize, revere, venerate

예 *Many Hindus worship Shiva.*

---

rule [rú:l]   규칙

图 a principle or condition that customarily governs behavior

图 government, norm, precept, principle, regulation

예 *Short haircuts were the rule.*

---

analyze [ǽnəlaiz]   분석하다

图 consider in detail and subject to an analysis in order to discover essential
   features or meaning

图 assay, test, decompose, construe, examine

예 *analyze the evidence in a criminal trial*

---

pat [pæt]   톡톡 치다

图 hit lightly

图 beat, clap, dab, stroke, tap

예 *pat him on the shoulder*

---

passive [pǽsiv]   수동적인

图 lacking in energy or will

图 compliant, inactive, inert, phlegmatic, submissive

예 *passive resister*

---

prevalent [prevələnt]   유행하는

图 most frequent or common

图 dominant, predominant, prevailing, rife, widespread

예 *prevailing winds*

---

flat [flǽt]   평평한

图 having a surface without slope, tilt in which no part is higher or lower than another

图 level, even, plain, plane, tabular

예 *skirts sewn with fine flat seams*

---

citizen [sítəzən]   시민

图 a native or naturalized member of a state or other political community

图 bourgeois, bourgeoisie, commoner, peasant, plebeian

예 *a law-abiding citizen*

---

similarly [símələrli]   유사하게

图 in like or similar manner

图 alike, correspondingly, ditto, equivalently, likewise

예 *He was similarly affected.*

increase [inkríːs]   늘다

图 make bigger or more

图 augment, enlarge, extend, grow, multiply

예 *The boss finally increased her salary.*

---

criticism [krítəsìzm]   비평, 비판

图 disapproval expressed by pointing out faults or shortcomings

图 animadversion, censure, critique, interpretation, review

예 *The senator received severe criticism from his opponent.*

*Vocabulary/Expressions

know [nóu] 알다

医 be cognizant or aware of a fact or a specific piece of information

동 appreciate, cognize, recognize, see, understand

예 *I know that the President lied to the people.*

disturb [distə:rb] 어지럽히다, 불안하게 하다

医 destroy the peace or tranquility of

동 interrupt, commove, bother, interfere, depress

예 *Don't disturb me when I'm reading*

interpret [intərprit] 해석하다

医 assign a meaning to

동 construe, explain, expound, render, translate

예 *What message do you interpret in this letter?*

polish [páliʃ] 윤이 나다

医 make a surface shine

동 burnish, furbish, gloss, shine, smoothen

예 *Polish the silver, please.*

depress [diprés] 낙담시키다

医 lower someone's spirits

동 deject, enervate, mortify, sadden, weaken

예 *These news depressed her.*

evident [évədənt] 분명한, 명백한

医 clearly revealed to the mind or the senses or judgment

동 apparent, manifest, obvious, plain, unmistakable

예 *evident hostility*

install [instɔːl] 　　　　　　　　　　　　　　　　　　설치하다

图 set up for use

圄 furnish, install, mount, set, settle

囘 *install the washer and dryer*

---

triumph [traiəmf] 　　　　　　　　　　　　　　　　　　승리

图 a successful ending of a struggle or contest

圄 achievement, success, triumph, victory, win

囘 *The general always gets credit for his army's triumph.*

---

reject [ridʒekt] 　　　　　　　　　　　　　　　　　　거절하다

图 refuse to accept or acknowledge

圄 decline, refuse, reprobate, spurn, veto

囘 *The journal rejected the student's paper.*

---

addictive [ədíktiv] 　　　　　　　　　　　　　　　　　습관성의

图 causing or characterized by addiction

圄 devoted, enslaving, habit-forming, hooking, obsessive

囘 *addictive behavior*

---

creep [kríːp] 　　　　　　　　　　　　　　　　　　　기다

图 move slowly

圄 crawl, glide, grovel, lurk, sneak

囘 *The crocodile was creeping along the riverbed.*

---

plane [pléin] 　　　　　　　　　　　　　　　　　　　편평한

图 having a surface without slope, tilt in which no part is higher or lower than another

圄 flat, horizontal, level, plain, smooth

囘 *a plane surface*

characterize [kǽriktəràiz]   특성을 기술하다

图 describe or portray the character or the qualities or peculiarities of

图 delineate, describe, feature, signalize, typify

예 *You can characterize his behavior as that of an egotist.*

---

emphasis [emfəsis]   강조

图 special importance or significance

图 accent, importance, intensity, prominence, strength

예 *the red light gave the central figure increased emphasis*

---

opportunity [ápərtjú:nəti]   기회

图 a possibility due to a favorable combination of circumstances

图 chance, circumstances, lucky, occasion, possibility

예 *The holiday gave us the opportunity to visit Washington.*

---

combat [kəmbǽt]   싸우다

图 battle or contend against in or as if in a battle

图 battle, contend, fight, struggle, wrestle

예 *The Kurds are combating Iraqi troops in Northern Iraq.*

---

merciful [mɛrsifəl]   자비로운

图 showing or giving mercy

图 charitable, compassionate, gracious, lenient, pitiful

예 *sought merciful treatment for the captives*

---

startle [stá:rtl]   깜짝 놀라게 하다

图 move or jump suddenly, as if in surprise or alarm

图 alarm, frighten, scare, surprise, terrify

예 *She startled when I walked into the room.*

---

poor [púər]   불쌍한

图 deserving or inciting pity

동 hapless, miserable, pathetic, piteous, wretched

예 *poor victims of war*

---

allow [əlau]   허락하다

图 consent to, give permission

동 accept, admit, concede, let, permit

예 *I cannot allow you to see your exam.*

---

limit [límit]   제한하다

图 restrict or confine

동 bound, circumscribe, confine, restrict, stint

예 *I limit you to two visits to the pub a day.*

---

conclusion [kənklúːʒən]   결말

图 a position or opinion or judgment reached after consideration

동 completion, decision, end, illation, termination

예 *a conclusion unfavorable to the opposition*

---

charity [tʃǽrəti]   자애

图 a kindly and lenient attitude toward people

동 alms, eneficence, benevolence, mercy, dole

예 *Charity begins at home.*

---

lower [lóuər]   낮추다

图 move something or somebody to a lower position

동 abate, diminish, drop, lour, reduce

예 *Lower the vase from the shelf.*

acquire [əkwàiər]   취득하다

- 图 come into the possession of something concrete or abstract
- 图 attain, get, obtain, procure, take
- 예 *They acquired a new pet.*

---

rural [rúərəl]   시골의

- 图 living in or characteristic of farming or country life
- 图 countrified, country, pastoral, rustic, village
- 예 *large rural households*

---

judge [dʒʌdʒ]   판단하다

- 图 form a critical opinion of
- 图 adjudicate, assess, decide, estimate, resolve
- 예 *How do you judge this grant proposal?*

---

plenty [plénti]   많음, 풍부

- 图 a large number or amount or extent
- 图 ample, abundant, copious, profusion, sufficiency
- 예 *see the rest of the winners in our plenty passel of photos*

---

surround [səràund]   둘러싸다

- 图 extend on all sides of simultaneously
- 图 beset, besiege, compass, encircle, gird
- 예 *The forest surrounds my property.*

---

remind [rimaind]   생각나게 하다, 상기시키다

- 图 put in the mind of someone
- 图 recall, remember, recollect, bethink
- 예 *Remind me to call Mother*

---

unfortunate [ʌnfɔːrtʃ ənət]   불운한

图 marked or accompanied by or resulting in ill fortune

통 hapless, infelicitous, luckless, unlucky, wretched

예 *an unfortunate turn of events*

---

rapid [rǽpid]   빠른

图 moving with or capable of moving with high speed

통 expeditious, fast, quick, speedy, swift

예 *a rapid errand boy*

---

instruct [instrʌkt]   가르치다

图 impart skills or knowledge to

통 educate, inform, learn, teach, train

예 *He instructed me in building a boat.*

---

genuine [dʒenjuin]   진짜의

图 sincerely felt or expressed

통 authentic, sincere, true, unfeigned, veritable

예 *Her interest in people was genuine.*

---

opponent [əpóunənt]   반대자

图 someone who offers opposition

통 antagonist, competitor, enemy, foe, rival

예 *generosity toward a defeated opponent*

---

perfect [pɜrfikt]   완전한图

being complete of its kind and without defect or blemish

통 complete, consummate, finished, flawless, thorough

예 *a perfect reproduction*

---

yield [jíːld]　　　　　　　　　　　　　　　　　　산출하다

圐 be the cause or source of

圏 afford, furnish, give, produce, provide

예 *Our meeting yielded much interesting information.*

---

expose [ikspouz]　　　　　　　　　　　　　　　드러내다

圐 to show, make visible or apparent

圏 disclose, display, present, reveal, unveil

예 *Why don't you expose your nice legs and wear shorter skirts.*

---

stare [stéər]　　　　　　　　　　　　　　　　응시하다

圐 look at with fixed eyes

圏 fix, gaze, goggle, peer, watch

예 *The students stared at the teacher with amazement.*

---

satisfied [sǽtisfàid]　　　　　　　　　　　　　　만족한

圐 filled with satisfaction

圏 contented, exhilarate, gratify, pleased, sate

예 *a satisfied customer*

---

devote [divóut]　　　　　　　　　　　　바치다, 헌신하다

圐 give entirely to a specific person, activity, or cause

圏 commit, consecrate, dedicate, entrust, give

예 *She devoted herself to the work of God.*

---

relieve [rilíːv]　　　　　　　　　　　　　　　경감하다

圐 lessen the intensity of or calm

圏 abate, alleviate, ease, mitigate, soothe

예 *The news relieved my conscience.*

homely [hóumli]   못생긴

图 lacking in physical beauty or proportion

图 disgusting, ordinary, ugly, unaesthetic, unattractive

예 *a homely child*

---

tenant [tenənt]   차용자

图 someone who pays rent to use land or a building or a car that is owned by someone else

图 holder, lessee, leaseholder, occupant, renter

예 *The landlord can evict a tenant who doesn't pay the rent.*

---

emphasize [émfəsàiz]   강조하다

图 to stress, single out as important

图 accentuate, punctuate, stress, underline, underscore

예 *Dr. Jones emphasizes exercise in addition to a change in diet.*

---

thorough [θɛ́rou]   철저한, 완전한

图 performed comprehensively and completely

图 careful, complete, entire, perfect, total

예 *made a thorough search*

---

depart [dipá:rt]   출발하다

图 move away from a place into another direction

图 emigrate, go, leave, migrate, start

예 *The train departs at noon.*

---

edition [idiʃən]   판

图 something a little different from others of the same type

图 issue, printing, publication, variant, version

예 *a edition of the same word*

---

aspect [ǽspekt]   외관

图 a distinct feature or element in a problem

图 appearance, facet, look, mien, side

예 *He studied every aspect of the question.*

---

valuable [vǽljuəbl]   귀중한

图 having worth or merit or value

图 beneficial, invaluable, precious, valued, worthy

예 *a valuable friend*

---

*Vocabulary/Expressions   Day 8

groundless [gràundlis]   근거없는
- 图 without a basis in reason or fact
- 图 baseless, causeless, gratuitous, unfounded, ungrounded
- 예 *groundless suspicions*

approximate [əpráksəmèit]   가까워지다
- 图 be close or similar
- 图 approach, border, near, reach, touch
- 예 *Her results approximate my own.*

study [stʌdi]   공부하다
- 图 consider in detail and subject to an analysis in order to discover essential features or meaning
- 图 analyze, canvass, examine, investigate, learn
- 예 *study the evidence in a criminal trial*

irritable [írətəbl]   화를 잘내는
- 图 easily irritated or annoyed
- 图 excitable, irascible, petulant, testy, touchy
- 예 *an incorrigibly irritable young man*

wealth [wélθ]   부, 재산
- 图 the state of being rich and affluent
- 图 affluence, fortune, mammon, opulence, richness
- 예 *Great wealth is not a sign of great intelligence.*

manipulate [mənípjulèit]   교묘하게 다루다
- 图 tamper, with the purpose of deception
- 图 fake, falsify, handle, operate, wangle
- 예 *manipulate the data*

dynamic [dainǽmik]   활동적인

뜻 characterized by action or forcefulness or force of personality

동 active, enterprising, lively, vehement, vital

예 *a dynamic market*

---

fairly [féərli]   상당히

뜻 to a moderately sufficient extent or degree

동 moderately, pretty, quite, somewhat, tolerably

예 *He is fairly clever with computers.*

---

misunderstanding [mìsʌndərstǽndiŋ]   오해

뜻 an understanding of something that is not correct

동 confusion, delusion, misapprehension, misconception, mistake

예 *He wasn't going to admit his misunderstanding.*

---

kindle [kíndl]   불붙이다

뜻 cause to start burning

동 conflagrate, enkindle, ignite, inflame, light

예 *The setting sun kindled the sky with oranges and reds.*

---

deficient [difíʃənt]   부족한

뜻 inadequate in amount or degree

동 faulty, insufficient, inadequate, scanty, wanting

예 *deficient in common sense*

---

stir [stɛr]   휘젓다

뜻 move an implement through

동 agitate, budge, mix, move, shake

예 *stir the soup*

magnitude [mǽgnətjùːd]   크기

图 the property of relative size or extent

동 bulk, dimension, extent, greatness, size

예 *They tried to predict the magnitude of the explosion.*

outdated [àutdéitid]   구식의

图 no longer valid or fashionable

동 antiquated, obsolete, outmoded, passe, superannuated

예 *an outdated locomotive*

transformation [trænsfərméiʃən]   변형

图 the act of changing in form or shape or appearance

동 alteration, conversion, metamorphosis, modification, transmutation

예 *A photograph is a translation of a scene onto a two-dimensional surface.*

equally [íːkwəli]   균등하게

图 in equal amounts or shares

동 alike, coequally, evenly, likewise, uniformly

예 *deal equally with rich and poor*

confused [kənfjúːzd]   혼란스러운

图 perplexed by many conflicting situations or statements

동 abashed, bewildered, disconcerted, embarrassed, perplexed

예 *obviously confused by his questions*

terrified [térəfàid]   무서워하는

图 thrown into a state of intense fear or desperation

동 aghast, alarmed, frightened, panicked, scared

예 *felt terrified before each exam*

soak [sóuk]   적시다
- 영 submerge in a liquid
- 동 absorb, drench, saturate, sop, wet
- 예 *I soaked in the hot tub for an hour.*

margin [máːrdʒin]   가장자리
- 영 the boundary line or the area immediately inside the boundary
- 동 border, edge, marge, rim, verge
- 예 *a wide margin*

vital [vàitl]   극히 중대한
- 영 urgently needed
- 동 cardinal, critical, essential, indispensable, prerequisite
- 예 *a vital element of the plan*

approach [əpróutʃ]   접근하다
- 영 move towards
- 동 approximate, border, converge, impend, surround
- 예 *We were approaching our destination.*

subject [sʌbdʒikt]   주제
- 영 the subject matter of a conversation or discussion
- 동 matter, motif, object, theme, topic
- 예 *He didn't want to discuss that subject.*

supervise [súːpərvàiz]   감독하다
- 영 watch and direct
- 동 control, inspect, monitor, oversee, watch
- 예 *Who is supervising this project?*

usually [júːʒuəli]   보통

㉅ under normal conditions

㊀ commonly, generally, normally, ordinarily, unremarkably

㉠ *Usually she was late.*

---

mood [múːd]   기분

㉅ a characteristic habitual or relatively temporary state of feeling

㊀ character, humor, individuality, spirit, temper

㉠ *He was in a bad mood.*

---

aboriginal [æbərídʒənl]   원주의, 토착의

㉅ characteristic of or relating to people inhabiting a region from the beginning

㊀ earliest, indigenous, native, primordial, primitive

㉠ *the aboriginal peoples of Australia*

---

candidate [kǽndidèit]   후보자, 지원자

㉅ someone who is considered for something (for an office or prize or honor etc.)

㊀ applicant, aspirant, nominee, postulant, seeker

㉠ *a presidential candidate*

---

stink [stíŋk]   악취를 풍기다

㉅ smell badly and offensively

㊀ mephitis, offend, reek, smell, stench

㉠ *The building stinks of smoke.*

---

dispose [dispóuz]   처리하다

㉅ throw or cast away

㊀ chuck, discard, fling, throw, toss

㉠ *Dispose your worries.*

tell [tél]
말하다

- 医 express in words
- 圄 narrate, recount, say, speak, state
- 예 *He told that he wanted to marry her.*

behavior [bihéivjər]
행동

- 医 the action or reaction of something under specified circumstances
- 圄 action, bearing, conduct, demeanor, manner
- 예 *The behavior of small particles can be studied in experiments.*

risk [rísk]
위험

- 医 a source of danger
- 圄 endangerment, hazard, jeopardy, menace, peril
- 예 *Drinking alcohol is a health risk.*

interpretation [intɛrprətei ʃ ən]
해석

- 医 an explanation of something that is not immediately obvious
- 圄 explanation, explication, reading, rendition, translation
- 예 *The edict was subject to many interpretations.*

straightforward [strèitfɔːrwərd]
정직한, 솔직한

- 医 without concealment or deception
- 圄 candid, forthright, frank, honest, outspoken
- 예 *straightforward in all his business affairs*

directly [diréktli]
곧장

- 医 without delay or hesitation
- 圄 anon, forthwith, immediately, instantly, straightway
- 예 *He answered directly.*

apologize [əpálədʒàiz]
사과하다
- 图 acknowledge faults or shortcomings or failing
- 图 atone, confess, purge, retract, withdraw
- 例 *I apologized for being late.*

experiment [ikspérəmənt]
실험
- 图 the testing of an idea
- 图 examination, investigation, research, test, trial
- 例 *It was an experiment in living.*

restoration [rèstəréiʃən]
회복
- 图 the state of being restored to its former good condition
- 图 cure, healing, recovery, renewal, restitution
- 例 *the restoration of order*

pressure [préʃər]
압박
- 图 a force that compels
- 图 compulsion, oppression, push, strain, tension
- 例 *The public brought pressure to bear on the government.*

horrific [hɔːrífik]
무서운
- 图 causing fear or dread or terror
- 图 dreadful, frightful, grisly, horrible, terrible
- 例 *the horrific presence of the headmaster*

attractive [ətrǽktiv]
매력적인
- 图 pleasing to the eye or mind especially through beauty or charm
- 图 alluring, charming, engaging, fetching, winsome
- 例 *an attractive personality*

misplaced [míspleist] 엉뚱한
圀 put in the wrong place or position
圐 confused, deranged, inappropriate, incoherent, unsettled
囫 *She was penalized for a spelling mistake or a misplaced accent.*

ancestor [ǽnsestər] 조상
圀 someone from whom you are descended
圐 father, forebear, forefather, primogenitor, progenitor
囫 *ancestor worship*

madden [mǽdn] 미치게 하다
圀 cause to go crazy
圐 annoy, craze, enrage, infuriate, pester
囫 *His behavior is maddening.*

deficiency [difíʃənsi] 부족
圀 lack of an adequate quantity or number
圐 absence, inadequacy, insufficiency, lack, shortage
囫 *the deficiency of unemployment benefits*

fake [féik] 속이다
圀 tamper, with the purpose of deception
圐 assume, falsify, feign, pretend, simulate
囫 *Fake the figures.*

encourage [inkə́ridʒ] 격려하다
圀 contribute to the progress or growth of
圐 advance, boost, further, promote, stimulate
囫 *I am encouraging the use of computers in the classroom.*

thereafter [ðὲərǽftər]　　　　　　　　　　　　　그 후에

图 from that time on

동 afterwards, subsequently, then, thenceforth, thereupon

예 *Thereafter he never called again.*

---

anxiety [æŋzàiəti]　　　　　　　　　　　　　　걱정

图 a relatively permanent state of worry and nervousness occurring in a variety of mental disorders

동 concern, inquietude, solicitude, tension, worry

예 *acute anxiety*

---

*Vocabulary/Expressions

Day 9

straight [stréit] 곧은
- 뜻 having no deviations
- 동 direct, erect, plain, right, upright
- 예 *straight shoulders*

spill [spíl] 엎지르다
- 뜻 cause or allow a liquid substance to run or flow from a container
- 동 drop, pour, shed, slop, splatter
- 예 *Spill the milk.*

absolute [ǽbsəlùːt] 완전한
- 뜻 perfect or complete or pure
- 동 complete, downright, perfect, plenary, sheer
- 예 *absolute loyalty*

essentiality [isènʃiǽləti] 본성, 본질
- 뜻 basic importance
- 동 character, essence, individuality, spirit, substance
- 예 *essentiality of human beings*

imagination [imædʒənéiʃən] 상상
- 뜻 the formation of a mental image of something that is not perceived as real and is not present to the senses
- 동 fancy, fantasy, idea, supposition, vision
- 예 *Imagination reveals what the world could be.*

fulfill [fulfil] 이행하다
- 뜻 fill or meet a want or need
- 동 accomplish, achieve, execute, perform, realize
- 예 *fulfill one's duties*

nurture [nɜrtʃər]   양육하다

图 provide with nourishment

图 educate, foster, instruct, nourish, nurse

예 *This kind of food is not nurturing for young children.*

---

render [réndər]   ~이 되게 하다

图 cause to become

图 contribute, give, make, translate, yield

예 *The shot rendered her immobile.*

---

board [bɔːrd]   판지

图 flat piece of material designed for a special purpose

图 panel, plank, slat, table, timber

예 *He nailed boards across the windows.*

---

apart [əpáːrt]   뿔뿔이

图 remote and separate physically or socially

图 aloof, aside, asunder, isolated, separately

예 *preserved because they inhabited a place apart*

---

faith [féiθ]   신념

图 a strong belief in a supernatural power or powers that control human destiny

图 belief, confidence, credence, reliance, trust

예 *He lost his faith but not his morality.*

---

considerable [kənsidərəbl]   상당한

图 large or relatively large in number or amount or extent or degree

图 important, notable, significant, sizable, substantial

예 *spent a considerable amount of time on the problem*

---

figure [fígjər] 나타나다

圆 see in one's mind

동 envision, image, picture, see, visualize

예 *I can figure a risk in this strategy.*

---

duration [djuréiʃən] 지속

圆 the property of enduring or continuing in time

동 continuance, endurance, perpetuation, prolongation, standing

예 *The ceremony was of short duration.*

---

demonstrate [demənstreit] 증명하다

圆 provide evidence for

동 attest, certify, evince, manifest, prove

예 *This decision demonstrates his sense of fairness.*

---

advantage [ædvǽntidʒ] 유리한 점

圆 the quality of having a superior or more favorable position

동 benefit, mastery, profit, supremacy, vantage

예 *The experience gave him the advantage over me.*

---

show [ʃóu] 보이다

圆 make visible or noticeable

동 display, indicate, manifest, present, reveal

예 *She showed her talent for cooking.*

---

aptitude [ǽptətju:d] 재능

圆 inherent ability

동 ability, capability, faculty, gift, talent

예 *have an aptitude for*

valueless [vǽlju:lis]   하찮은

뜻 of no value

동 ineffective, nugatory, unworthy, useless, worthless

예 *valueless object*

---

cheer [tʃíər]   격려하다

뜻 cause somebody to feel happier or more cheerful

동 acclaim, applaud, comfort, encourage, gladden

예 *She tried to cheer up the disappointed child when he failed to win the spelling bee.*

---

identify [aidéntəfài]   확인하다

뜻 establish the identity of someone or something

동 confirm, discover, distinguish, find, recognize

예 *She identified the man on the 'wanted' poster.*

---

conduct [kándʌkt]   행동하다

뜻 behave in a certain manner

동 act, behave, comport, manage, take

예 *They conducted themselves well during these difficult times.*

---

creature [krí:tʃər]   생물

뜻 a living organism characterized by voluntary movement

동 being, creation, fauna, person, thing

예 *a creature of fancy*

---

halfway [hǽfwèi]   중간의

뜻 at half the distance

동 intermediate, midway, moderate, partial, partly

예 *He was halfway down the ladder when he fell.*

clothes [klóuz] 옷

뜻 clothing in general

동 apparel, clothing, dress, garb, raiment

예 *He always bought his clothes at the same store.*

---

grain [gréin] 곡물

뜻 a cereal grass

동 cereal, corn, granule, kernel, seed

예 *wheat is a grain that is grown in Kansas.*

---

sore [sɔːr] 아픈

뜻 hurting

동 aching, distressing, irritated, painful, raw

예 *the sore spot on his jaw*

---

decorate [dékərèit] 장식하다

뜻 make more attractive by adding ornament, color, etc

동 adorn, bedeck, embellish, garnish, trim

예 *Decorate the room for the party.*

---

disagreement [dìsəgrí:mənt] 불일치, 의견차이

뜻 a difference between conflicting facts or claims or opinions

동 discordance, dissent, opposition, quarrel, wrangle

예 *a growing disagreement of opinion*

---

decent [dí:snt] 점잖은

뜻 according with custom or propriety

동 decorous, modest, proper, respectable, seemly

예 *decent behavior*

crime [kràim]   죄

图 usually considered an evil act

图 felony, guilt, misdeed, offence, sin

예 *a long record of crimes*

---

impose [impouz]   강요하다

图 compel to behave in a certain way

图 ask, enforce, extort, force, inflict

예 *Social relations impose courtesy.*

---

aged [éidʒid]   노령의

图 advanced in years

图 age-old, elderly, gray, older, senior

예 *Aged residents could remember the construction of the first skyscraper.*

---

indicate [índikèit]   나타내다

图 be a signal for or a symptom of

图 denote, designate, show, signify, suggest

예 *The economic indicators signal that the euro is undervalued.*

---

qualification [kwàləfikeiʃən]   자격

图 an attribute that must be met or complied with and that fits a person for
something

图 ability, aptitude, capability, fitness, reservation

예 *Her qualifications for the job are excellent.*

---

urge [ɛrdʒ]   강요하다

图 force or impel in an indicated direction

图 compel, exhort, impel, press, spur

예 *I urged him to finish his studies.*

---

stimulating [stímjulèitiŋ]   자극하는

園 rousing or quickening activity or the senses

동 appealing, excitant, inspiring, stimulant, stirring

예 *a stimulating discussion*

---

majority [mədʒɔːrəti]   대부분

園 the property resulting from being or relating to the greater in number of two parts

동 bulk, most, plurality, preponderance, superiority

예 *The majority of his customers prefer it.*

---

mode [móud]   방법

園 how something is done or how it happens

동 manner, method, modus, style, way

예 *her dignified mode*

---

sum [sʌm]   합계

園 the whole amount

동 aggregate, amount, number, total, whole

예 *the sum and total*

---

dismay [disméi]   당황케 하다

園 fill with apprehension or alarm

동 appal, horrify, frighten, scare, terrify

예 *The news of the executions dismayed us.*

---

priceless [práislis]   아주 귀중한

園 having incalculable monetary, intellectual, or spiritual worth

동 inappreciable, inestimable, invaluable, precious, treasured

예 *a priceless friend*

---

culture [kʌltʃər] 문화
图 a particular society at a particular time and place
图 civilization, cultivation, customs, enlightenment, lifestyle
예 *early Mayan culture*

happen [hǽpən] 일어나다
图 happen, occur, or be the case in the course of events or by chance
图 bechance, befall, come, occur, transpire
예 *It happens that today is my birthday.*

evaluate [ivǽljuèit] 평가하다
图 evaluate or estimate the nature, quality, ability, extent, or significance of
图 appraise, assess, estimate, measure, valuate
예 *I will have the family jewels evaluated by a professional*

saddle [sǽdl] (책임을) 지우다
图 impose a task upon, assign a responsibility to
图 burden, charge, load, tax, weight
예 *He saddled her with cleaning up all the files over the weekend.*

chop [tʃáp] 자르다
图 cut into pieces
图 cleave, divide, hack, lop, sever
예 *Chop wood*

dizzy [dízi] 현기증나는
图 having or causing a whirling sensation
图 confused, giddy, puzzled, vertiginous, woozy
예 *a dizzy pinnacle*

component [kəmpounənt]   구성요소

图 something determined in relation to something that includes it

통 constituent, element, factor, ingredient, part

예 *I read a component of the manuscript.*

---

reaction [riǽk ʃ ən]   반응

图 a response that reveals a person's feelings or attitude

통 answer, feedback, reflection, reply, response

예 *He was pleased by the audience's reaction to his performance.*

---

*Vocabulary/Expressions

overwhelming [òuvərhwélmiŋ]   압도적인

㈜ so strong as to be irresistible

㈜ amazing, crushing, intense, overpowering, vast

㈜ *an overpowering need for solitude*

---

delightful [diláitfəl]   매우 기쁜

㈜ greatly pleasing or entertaining

㈜ agreeable, delectable, gratifying, pleasant, scrumptious

㈜ *a delightful surprise*

---

conceive [kənsí:v]   상상하다

㈜ have the idea for

㈜ believe, consider, fancy, imagine, think

㈜ *He conceived of a robot that would help paralyzed patients.*

---

revenge [rivéndʒ]   복수하다

㈜ to inflict harm in return for, as an injury, insult, etc

㈜ avenge, defend, punish, reprisal, retaliate

㈜ *He wants to revenge the murder of his brother*

---

successful [səksésfəl]   성공한

㈜ having succeeded or being marked by a favorable outcome

㈜ advantageous, lucky, fortunate, outstanding, prosperous

㈜ *a successful architect*

---

imaginative [imǽdʒənətiv]   상상의

㈜ marked by independence and creativity in thought or action

㈜ creative, dreamy, fanciful, inventive, visionary

㈜ *an imaginative use of material*

85

ensure [inʃúər]   확실하게하다
- 医 be careful or certain to do something
- 동 assure, confirm, guarantee, indemnify, secure
- 예 *He ensured that the valves were closed.*

formation [fɔ:rméiʃən]   형성
- 医 the act of forming or establishing something
- 동 composition, constitution, embodiment, establishment, makeup
- 예 *It was the formation of his reputation.*

currency [kɛrənsi]   통화, 유통
- 医 general acceptance or use
- 동 cash, circulation, dollar, money, notes
- 예 *the currency of ideas*

fragrant [fréigrənt]   향기로운
- 医 pleasant-smelling
- 동 aromatic, balmy, odorous, perfumed, scented
- 예 *a fragrant tulip*

flutter [flʌtər]   펄럭이다
- 医 *move along rapidly and lightly*
- 동 flicker, flap, fly, quiver, wave
- 예 *The hummingbird fluttered among the branches.*

push [púʃ]   밀다
- 医 move with force
- 동 force, jostle, press, shove, thrust
- 예 *He pushed the table into a corner.*

enlighten [inlàitn]   설명하다

圐 make understand

동 elucidate, explain, inculcate, inform

예 *Can you enlighten me? I don't understand this proposal.*

benefit [bénəfit]   이익

圐 something that aids or promotes well-being

동 advantage, avail, favor, profit, worth

예 *for the benefit of all*

response [rispáns]   응답

圐 a statement that is made to reply to a question or request or criticism or accusation

동 answer, antiphon, rejoinder, replication, reply

예 *I waited several days for his answer.*

manner [mǽnər]   방법

圐 how something is done or how it happens

동 approach, method, mode, process, way

예 *her dignified manner*

interesting [íntərəstiŋ]   흥미있는

圐 arousing or holding the attention

동 amusing, entertaining, impressive, riveting, sapid

예 *an interesting books*

retreat [ritrí:t]   퇴각

圐 withdrawal of troops to a more favorable position to escape the enemy's superior forces or after a defeat

동 refuge, recession, retirement, shelter, withdrawal

예 *the disorderly retreat of French troops*

rub [rʌb]   비비다
- 图 move over something with pressure
- 图 chafe, fray, scrape, scratch, wipe
- 예 *Rub my hands.*

broad [brɔːd]   널따란
- 图 having great extent from one side to the other
- 图 extensive, large, spacious, vast, wide
- 예 *a broad river*

confusing [kənfjúːziŋ]   혼란시키는
- 图 causing confusion or disorientation
- 图 befuddling, confounding, disconcerting, perplexing, puzzling,
- 예 *a confusing jumble of road signs*

remove [rimúːv]   제거하다
- 图 dispose of
- 图 abolish, discard, eliminate, expunge, throw
- 예 *Remove these old shoes.*

thus [ðʌs]   그러므로
- 图 from that fact or reason or as a result
- 图 accordingly, consequently, hence, so, therefore
- 예 *The eggs were fresh and thus satisfactory.*

section [sek ʃ ən]   부분
- 图 one of several parts or pieces that fit with others to constitute a whole object
- 图 department, division, part, portion, segment
- 예 *a section of a fishing rod*

escape [iskéip]   도망하다

뜻 remove oneself from a familiar environment, usually for pleasure or diversion

동 avoid, elude, evade, flee, run

예 *We escaped to our summer house for a few days.*

misleading [mislí:diŋ]   오해시키는

뜻 designed to deceive or mislead either deliberately or inadvertently

동 deceptive, delusive, fallacious, false, illusive

예 *deliberately misleading packaging*

almost [ɔ:lmoust]   거의

뜻 slightly short of or not quite accomplished

동 approximately, most, nearly, practically, roughly

예 *The recording is almost perfect.*

expert [ekspə:rt]   전문가

뜻 a person with special knowledge or ability who performs skillfully

동 adept, connoisseur, master, proficient, specialist

예 *an acknowledged recognized expert*

eliminate [iliməneit]   제거하다

뜻 terminate, end, or take out

동 annihilate, eradicate, reject, remove, terminate

예 *eliminate my debts*

hence [héns]   그러므로

뜻 from that fact or reason or as a result

동 accordingly, consequently, therefore, thus, so

예 *It is late and hence we must go.*

extinct [ikstiŋkt]   사라진

뜻 no longer in existence

동 dead, defunct, nonextant, obsolete, vanished

예 *extinct laws and customs*

---

legal [líːgəl]   합법적인

뜻 having legal efficacy or force

동 juridical, lawful, legitimate, rightful, statutory

예 *a legal title to the property*

---

locate [lóukeit]   거처를 정하다

뜻 determine the place of

동 place, position, set, settle, situate

예 *Can you locate your cousins in the Midwest?*

---

describe [diskràib]   묘사하다

뜻 to give an account or representation of in words

동 characterize, depict, draw, portray, represent

예 *He described an elaborate plan of attack.*

---

break [bréik]   깨뜨리다

뜻 become separated into pieces or fragments

동 crack, fracture, separate, shatter, smash

예 *The figurine broke.*

---

oppose [əpouz]   반대하다

뜻 express opposition to

동 dissent, object, resist, thwart, withstand

예 *We oppose the ban on abortion.*

requirement [rikwàiərmənt]   요구

图 required activity

图 claim, demand, request, requisition, urgency

예 *The requirements of his work affected his health.*

---

device [diváis]   장치

图 an instrumentality invented for a particular purpose

图 apparatus, contrivance, gadget, instrument, scheme

예 *A device intended to conserve water.*

---

distinguish [distiŋgwiʃ]   구별하다

图 mark as different

图 characterize, differentiate, discern, discriminate, separate

예 *We distinguish several kinds of maple.*

---

batter [bǽtər]   난타하다

图 strike violently and repeatedly

图 baste, beat, clobber, pummel, strike

예 *She battered the man who tried to attack her.*

---

arrange [əréindʒ]   배열하다

图 put into a proper or systematic order

图 array, dispose, order, organize, settle

예 *Arrange the books on the shelves in chronological order.*

---

anticipate [æntisəpeit]   예상하다

图 regard something as probable or likely

图 expect, forebode, foresee, predict, previse

예 *The meteorologists are expecting rain for tomorrow.*

---

productivity [pròudʌktívəti]   생산성
뜻 the quality of being productive or having the power to produce
동 efficiency, fertility, output, productiveness, yield
예 *labor productivity*

---

famine [fǽmin]   기근
뜻 an acute insufficiency
동 dearth, hunger, scarcity, shortage, starvation
예 *a feast or a famine*

---

urban [ə́rbən]   도시의
뜻 relating to or concerned with a city or densely populated area
동 burghal, city, downtown, municipal, oppidan
예 *urban development*

---

omit [oumit]   생략하다
뜻 prevent from being included or considered or accepted
동 drop, miss, neglect, overlook, skip
예 *The bad results were omitted from the report.*

---

compliment [kámpləmənt]   칭찬하다
뜻 say something to someone that expresses praise
동 commend, congratulate, felicitate, laud, praise
예 *He complimented her on her last physics paper.*

---

dissatisfied [dissǽtisfàid]   불만스러운
뜻 in a state of sulky dissatisfaction
동 discontented, displeased, malcontent, uncontented, unsatisfied
예 *a dissatisfied look*

plethora [pléθərə]   과잉

图 extreme excess

동 embarrassment, glut, overplus, superabundance, superfluity

예 *an plethora of riches*

---

correspond [kɔ:rəspánd]   일치하다

图 be compatible, similar or consistent

동 accord, assimilate, coincide, fit, match

예 *The two stories don't correspond in many details.*

---

*Vocabulary/Expressions

Day 11

factor [fǽktər]   요인

囲 anything that contributes causally to a result

同 cause, component, determinant, item, part

예 *A number of factors determined the outcome.*

---

travel [trǽvəl]   여행하다

囲 travel upon or across

同 jaunt, journey, peregrinate, tour, voyage

예 *Travel the oceans.*

---

remindful [rimàindfəl]   생각나게 하는

囲 serving to bring to mind

同 evocative, implicative, redolent, reminiscent, suggestive

예 *a campaign remindful of machine politics*

---

eventually [ivéntʃuəli]   결국

囲 after an unspecified period of time or an especially long delay

同 after all, at last, finally, lastly, ultimately

예 *Eventually he had to give in.*

---

keep [kíːp]   유지하다

囲 continue a certain state, condition, or activity

同 continue, hold, maintain, proceed, retain

예 *Keep on working!*

---

reconciliation [rèkənsìliéiʃən]   조화, 일치

囲 getting two things to correspond

同 adaptation, balancing, compromise, fitting, settlement

예 *the reconciliation of his checkbook and the bank statement*

sensible [sénsəbl]   분별있는

图 aware intuitively or intellectually of something sensed

图 judicious, perceptible, rational, reasonable, wise

예 *made sensible of his mistakes*

---

owing [óuiŋ]   빚지고 있는

图 owed as a debt

图 due, indebted, outstanding, owing, undischarged

예 *owing bills*

---

undeniable [ʌndinàiəbl]   부정하기 어려운

图 not possible to deny

图 incontestable, incontrovertible, indisputable, irrefutable, unquestionable

예 *an undeniable fact*

---

subscribe [səbskràib]   기부하다

图 pay an amount of money as a contribution to a charity or service

图 consent, donate, grant, pledge, support

예 *I subscribed $10 a month to my favorite radio station.*

---

narration [næréiʃən]   이야기

图 a message that tells the particulars of an act or occurrence or course of events

图 account, description, narrative, story, tale

예 *His narrative was interesting.*

---

remark [rimá:rk]   논평하다

图 make or write a comment on

图 comment, commentate, note, observe, review

예 *He remarked the paper of his colleague.*

Day 11

install [instɔːl]   설치하다

图 set up for use

图 furnish, install, mount, set, settle

예 *install the washer and dryer*

---

innocent [ínəsənt]   순진한

图 lacking in sophistication or worldliness

图 ingenuous, naive, pure, sincere, unsophisticated

예 *a child's innocent stare*

---

content [kántent]   내용

图 everything that is included in a collection and that is held or included in something

图 essence, idea, matter, meaning, substance

예 *He emptied the contents of his pockets.*

---

principle [prínsəpl]   원칙

图 a rule or law concerning a natural phenomenon or the function of a complex system

图 basis, law, rule, standard, tenet

예 *the principle of the conservation of mass*

---

effort [éfərt]   노력

图 earnest and conscientious activity intended to do or accomplish something

图 attempt, endeavor, exertion, labor, try

예 *made an effort to cover all the reading material*

---

suggest [səgdʒest]   제의하다

图 make a proposal, declare a plan for something

图 advise, imply, propound, propose, recommend

예 *The senator suggested to abolish the sales tax.*

essay [ései]   시도하다

图 make an effort or attempt

동 assay, attempt, endeavor, seek, try

예 *The infant had essayed a few wobbly steps.*

---

personal [pɑːrsənl]   개인의

图 concerning or affecting a particular person or his or her private life and personality

동 individual, own, particular, private, subjective

예 *for your personal use*

---

forecast [fɔːrkæst]   예보하다

图 predict in advance

동 anticipate, foretell, predict, presage, prognosticate

예 *forecast the weather*

---

convert [kənvɛrt]   전환하다

图 change from one system to another or to a new plan or policy

동 alter, change, transform, transmute, turn

예 *We converted from 220 to 110 Volt.*

---

reserve [rizɛrv]   예약하다

图 arrange for and reserve (something for someone else) in advance

동 bespeak, book, engage, hold, preengage

예 *The agent reserved tickets to the show for the whole family.*

---

tension [ténʃən]   긴장

图 a state of mental or emotional strain or suspense

동 strain, stress, tenseness, tensity, tightness

예 *He suffered from fatigue and emotional tension.*

---

block [blák]　　　　　　　　　　　　　　　　　　　　막다

圏 stop from happening or developing

圄 bar, blockade, embarrass, hinder, obstruct

囫 *Block his election.*

---

intensive [inténsiv]　　　　　　　　　　　　　　격렬한

圏 characterized by a high degree or intensity

圄 concentrated, hard, intense, profound, severe

囫 *intensive conditions*

---

pave [péiv]　　　　　　　　　　　　　　　　　　포장하다

圏 cover with a material such as stone or concrete to make suitable for vehicle traffic

圄 cobble, concrete, cover, macadamize, superimpose

囫 *pave the roads in the village*

---

garbage [gá:rbidʒ]　　　　　　　　　　　　　　쓰레기

圏 food that is discarded as from a kitchen

圄 junk, litter, offal, rubbish, trash

囫 *garbage can*

---

retire [ritaiər]　　　　　　　　　　　　퇴직하다, 은퇴하다

圏 stop performing one's work or withdraw from one's position

圄 recede, stop working, regress, repeal, retreat

囫 *He retired at age 68*

---

complain [kəmplein]　　　　　　　　　　　　　불평하다

圏 express complaints, discontent, displeasure, or unhappiness

圄 grumble, lament, moan, repine, protest

囫 *My mother complains all day.*

resent [rizént]   분개하다

图 feel bitter or indignant about

图 abhor, detest, grudge, irritate, scorn

예 *She resents being paid less than her co-workers.*

account [əkaunt]   계산, 셈, 회계

图 a statement of recent transactions and the resulting balance

图 reckoning, computation, tally, bill

예 *They send me an account every month.*

respond [rispánd]   대답하다

图 react verbally

图 answer, reply, rejoin, react, return

예 *We responded that we would accept the invitation.*

retirement [ritàiərmənt]   은퇴

图 the state of being retired from one's business or occupation

图 pullout, retreat, seclusion, superannuation, withdrawal

예 *early retirement*

melt [mélt]   녹다

图 reduce or cause to be reduced from a solid to a liquid state, usually by heating

图 deliquesce, dissolve, fuse, liquefy, thaw

예 *The wax melted in the sun.*

employ [implɔi]   쓰다, 고용하다

图 engage or hire for work

图 apply, engage, hire, use, utilize

예 *They hired two new secretaries in the department.*

academic [ə kədémik]
학구적인, 이론적인

医 hypothetical or theoretical and not expected to produce an immediate or practical result

동 erudite, scholastic, studious, theoretical, theoretic

예 *an academic discussion*

transfer [trænsfɛr]
옮기다, 나르다, 건네다

医 move from one place to another

동 shift, relocate, displace, carry, transport

예 *transfer the data*

still [stíl]
조용한

医 marked by absence of sound

동 noiseless, quiet, silent, soundless, tranquil

예 *a still house*

mumble [mʌmbl]
중얼거리다

医 talk indistinctly, usually in a low voice

동 babble, grumble, mutter, murmur, whine

예 *mumble the answer*

nearby [níərbài]
가까운

医 close at hand

동 adjacent, adjoining, close, neighboring, proximate

예 *the nearby towns*

deny [dinai]
부정하다

医 refuse to recognize or acknowledge

동 disaffirm, disclaim, negate, refuse, reject

예 *Peter denied Jesus.*

unresolved [ʌnrizálvd]　　　　　　　　결심이 서지 않은
- 뜻 not brought to a conclusion
- 동 indecisive, irresolute, undecided, unsettled, unsolved
- 예 *Position on this bill is still unresolved.*

disappear [dìsəpíər]　　　　　　　　사라지다
- 뜻 become invisible or unnoticeable
- 동 abscond, expire, evanesce, vanish, wane
- 예 *The effect disappeared when day broke.*

reconsider [rì:kənsídər]　　　　　　　재고하다
- 뜻 consider again
- 동 amend, correct, polish, review, revise
- 예 *Won't you reconsider your decision?*

previous [pri:viəs]　　　　　　　　이전의
- 뜻 just preceding something else in time or order
- 동 anterior, foregoing, former, precedent, prior
- 예 *the previous owner*

generally [dʒénərəli]　　　　　　　일반적으로
- 뜻 usually as a rule
- 동 commonly, in general, ordinarily, mostly, usually
- 예 *Generally it doesn't rain much here.*

expand [ikspǽnd]　　　　　　　　넓히다
- 뜻 extend in one or more directions
- 동 amplify, augment, extend, magnify, spread
- 예 *The dough expands.*

sharply [ʃ á:rpli]

급격하게

뜻 changing suddenly in direction and degree

동 acutely, discernibly, pointedly, precipitously, strongly

예 *The road twists sharply after the light.*

decentralize [di:sentrəlaiz]

분산시키다

뜻 make less central

동 deconcentrate, diffract, disject, dispersion, separate

예 *After the revolution, food distribution was decentralized.*

*Vocabulary/Expressions

Day 12

vague [veig]
막연한
圀 not clearly understood or expressed
圄 ambiguous, equivocal, indistinct, obscure, tenebrous
囮 *an vague turn of phrase*

active [ǽktiv]
활동적인
圀 characterized by energetic activity
圄 brisk, energetic, lively, operative, shifting
囮 *an active toddler*

consequently [kánsəkwèntli]
그 결과
圀 because of the reason given
圄 accordingly, hence, so, therefore, thus
囮 *Consequently, he didn't do it.*

disastrous [dizǽstrəs]
비참한
圀 having extremely unfortunate or dire consequences
圄 calamitous, catastrophic, fatal, pernicious, unfortunate
囮 *The battle was a disastrous end to a disastrous campaign.*

agreement [əgri:mənt]
일치
圀 harmony of people's opinions or actions or characters
圄 accord, accordance, concord, concordance, harmony
囮 *The two parties were in agreement.*

superior [səpiəriər]
뛰어난
圀 of high or superior quality or performance
圄 distinguished, excellent, predominant, remarkable, surpassing
囮 *Superior wisdom derived from experience.*

auditory [ɔ:dətɔ:ri]   귀의, 청각의

圐 of or relating to the process of hearing

圄 acoustic, audile, auditive, aural, auricular

例 *auditory processing*

---

gradually [grǽdʒuəli]   차차

圐 in a gradual manner

圄 bit by bit, piecemeal, progressively, slowly, step by step

例 *The snake moved gradually toward its victim.*

---

fluffy [flʌfi]   푹신한

圐 like down or as soft as down

圄 downlike, downy, flossy, fuzzy, linty

例 *The bedding is soft and fluffy.*

---

transform [trænsfɔ:rm]   변형시키다

圐 change or alter in form, appearance, or nature

圄 transmute, transubstantiate, convert, mutate, transfigure

例 *transformed the clay into a beautiful sculpture*

---

portion [pɔ:r ʃ ən]   부분

圐 something determined in relation to something that includes it

圄 component, part, piece, quota, segment

例 *I read a portion of the manuscript*

---

organization [ɔ:rgənizei ʃ ən]   조직(화), 구성, 편성

圐 a group of people who work together

圄 assembly, institution, constitution, system, unity

例 *nongovernmental organization*

---

robber [rάbər] 강도, 도둑

图 a thief who steals from someone by threatening violence

圄 bandit, burglar, mugger, plunderer, thief

예 *a robber band*

---

appeal [əpíːl] 호소하다

图 ask for aid or protection

圄 beseech, crave, invoke, plead, solicit

예 *appeal to somebody for help*

---

resort [rizɔːrt] 행락지

图 a frequently visited place

圄 camp, harbor, haunt, lodge, spa

예 *seaside resort*

---

distort [distɔːrt] 왜곡하다

图 make false by mutilation or addition

圄 contort, deform, garble, pervert, warp

예 *distort history*

---

grind [grάind] 갈다, 빻다

图 reduce to small pieces or particles by pounding or abrading

圄 comminute, crunch, mash, mill, whet

예 *Grind the spices in a mortar.*

---

awesome [ɔːsəm] 무시무시한

图 inspiring awe or admiration or wonder

圄 amazing, awful, dreadful, formidable, horrible

예 *the awesome complexity of the universe*

Day 12

depressed [diprést]   의기소침한

图 filled with melancholy and despondency

图 dejected, despondent, dispirited, gloomy, sad

예 *depressed by the loss of his job*

graceful [gréisfəl]   우아한

图 suggesting taste, ease, and wealth

图 charming, elegant, exquisite, refined, tasteful

예 *her graceful movements*

positive [pázətiv]   명확한

图 characterized by or displaying affirmation or acceptance or certainty etc.

图 absolute, affirmative, certain, definite, sure

예 *a positive attitude*

stick [stík]   찌르다

图 put, fix, force, or implant

图 impale, insert, penetrate, pierce, thrust

예 *Stick your thumb in the crack.*

countless [kauntlis]   셀 수 없는, 무수한

图 too numerous to be counted

图 numberless, infinite, uncounted, innumerable, innumerous

예 *countless hours*

exist [igzíst]   존재하다

图 have an existence, be extant

图 abide, be, dwell, live, subsist

예 *cease to exist*

material [mətíəriəl]　　　　　　　　　　　　재료, 물질

圈 the tangible substance that goes into the makeup of a physical object

圈 cloth, fabric, matter, stuff, substance

圈 *Wheat is the material they use to make bread.*

trigger [trígər]　　　　　　　　　　　　유발하다

圈 put in motion or move to act

圈 activate, cause, elicit, generate, produce

圈 *trigger a reaction*

discover [diskʌvər]　　　　　　　　　　발견하다

圈 get to know or become aware of, usually accidentally

圈 detect, disclose, find, notice, unearth

圈 *She detected high levels of lead in her drinking water.*

public [pʌblik]　　　　　　　　　　　　공공의

圈 open to or concerning the people as a whole

圈 common, communal, general, national, popular

圈 *public libraries*

flatter [flǽtər]　　　　　　　　　　　　아첨하다

圈 praise somewhat dishonestly

圈 adulate, blandish, blarney, cajole, wheedle

圈 *a flattering remark*

stay [stéi]　　　　　　　　　　　　머무르다

圈 remain in a certain state

圈 abide, keep, remain, rest, stand

圈 *stay alone*

intricate [íntrikət]   복잡한

뜻 having many complexly arranged elements

동 complicated, elaborate, involute, knotty, tangly

예 *intricate lacework*

---

circumstance [sə́ːrkəmstæns]   상황

뜻 a condition that accompanies or influences some event or activity

동 case, condition, fact, occasion, situation

예 *the historical context*

---

conquer [káŋkər]   정복하다

뜻 take possession of by force, as after an invasion

동 capture, defeat, seize, subjugate, vanquish

예 *The militia conquered the castle.*

---

sparkling [spáːrkliŋ]   빛나는

뜻 shining with brilliant points of light like stars

동 brilliant, glittering, shining, shiny, twinkling

예 *sparkling eyes*

---

sort [sɔːrt]   종류

뜻 a category of things distinguished by some common characteristic or quality

동 category, class, kind, species, type

예 *sculpture is a sort of art*

---

frightened [fràitnd]   깜짝놀란

뜻 thrown into a state of intense fear or desperation

동 afraid, dismayed, fearful, scared, terrified

예 *The frightened horse bolted.*

mindful [màindfəl]   유념하는

㊉ bearing in mind

㊂ attentive, careful, observant, regardful, thoughtful

㊃ *mindful of his responsibilities*

---

insulation [insəléiʃən]   분리, 격리

㊉ the state of being isolated or detached

㊂ detachment, isolation, seclusion, segregation, separation

㊃ *The insulation of England was preserved by the English Channel.*

---

narrow [nǽrou]   폭이 좁은

㊉ not wide

㊂ close, limited, parochial, strait, tight

㊃ *a narrow line across the page*

---

offense [əféns]   위반

㊉ an act punishable by law

㊂ crime, misdemeanor, offence, transgression, trespass

㊃ *a long record of offenses*

---

individual [ìndəvídʒuəl]   개인의

㊉ concerning one person exclusively

㊂ particular, person, private, self, single

㊃ *We all have individual cars.*

---

portray [pɔːrtréi]   묘사하다

㊉ assume or act the character of

㊂ delineate, depict, describe, limn, represent

㊃ *The actor portrays an elderly, lonely man.*

assume [əsuːm]   추정하다

뜻 take to be the case or to be true

동 infer, presuppose, presume, suppose, take

예 *I assume his train was late.*

amuse [əmjúːz]   재미있게 하다

뜻 make somebody laugh

동 entertain, divert, recreate, regale, tickle

예 *The clown amused the children.*

vertical [vɜːrtikəl]   수직의

뜻 at right angles to the plane of the horizon or a base line

동 erect, perpendicular, plumb, sheer, upright

예 *Measure the vertical height.*

scholarly [skálərli]   학구적인

뜻 characteristic of scholars or scholarship

동 academic, erudite, learned, lettered, scientific

예 *scholarly pursuits*

adapt [ədǽpt]   적응시키다

뜻 adapt or conform oneself to new or different conditions

동 accommodate, adjust, conform, fit, suit

예 *We must adapt to the bad economic situation.*

challenging [tʃǽlindʒiŋ]   도전적인

뜻 requiring full use of your abilities or resources

동 ambitious, arduous, defiant, provocative, strenuous

예 *Performed the most challenging task without a mistake.*

dig [díg]   파헤치다

- 뜻 turn up, loosen, or remove earth
- 동 delve, excavate, grub, penetrate, unearth
- 예 *dig the soil for aeration*

---

state [stéit]   상태

- 뜻 the way something is with respect to its main attributes
- 동 circumstance, condition, position, status, situation
- 예 *in a weak financial state*

---

*Vocabulary/Expressions   Day 13

---

sentence [séntəns]   선고하다
- 图 pronounce a sentence on somebody in a court of law
- 图 adjudge, condemn, convict, doom, judge
- 예 *He was condemned to ten years in prison.*

---

prosper [práspər]   번영하다
- 图 make steady progress
- 图 bloom, flourish, progress, succeed, thrive
- 예 *enjoy prosperity*

---

evolution [evəlu:ʃən]   발달
- 图 a process in which something passes by degrees to a different stage
- 图 development, evolvement, growth, progress, transformation
- 예 *the evolution of Greek civilization*

---

quack [kwǽk]   꽥꽥 울다
- 图 utter quacking noises
- 图 babble, blather, cackle, gibber, snigger
- 예 *The ducks quacked.*

---

manual [mǽnjuəl]   소책자, 취급 설명서, 편람, 안내서
- 图 a small handbook
- 图 guidebook, enchiridion, instruction
- 예 *see manual*

---

incredible [inkredəbl]   놀라운
- 图 beyond belief or understanding
- 图 fabulous, improbable, inconceivable, unbelievable, unlikely
- 예 *The book's plot is simply incredible.*

---

autograph [ɔ:təgræf]
서명하다

图 mark with one's signature

图 endorse, handwrite, inscribe, sign, subscribe

예 *The author autographed his book.*

---

enlargement [inlá:rdʒmənt]
확대

图 the act of increasing something in size or volume or quantity or scope

图 amplification, expansion, extension, increment, magnification

예 *make an enlargement of a photograph*

---

devotion [divóuʃən]
헌신

图 feelings of ardent love

图 adherence, dedication, fidelity, loyalty, piety

예 *Their devotion to each other was beautiful.*

---

disease [dizí:z]
병

图 an impairment of health or a condition of abnormal functioning

图 ailment, distemper, illness, malady, pathosis

예 *a serious disease*

---

frustrate [frʌstreit]
좌절시키다

图 hinder or prevent (the efforts, plans, or desires) of

图 thwart, disappoint, discourage, dishearten, obstruct

예 *What ultimately frustrated every challenger was Ruth's amazing September surge*

---

burst [bə:rst]
터지다

图 force out or release suddenly and often violently something pent up

图 break, crack, erupt, explode, spout

예 *burst into tears*

disastrous [dizǽstrəs]   비참한

뜻 having extremely unfortunate or dire consequences

동 calamitous, catastrophic, devastating, fatal, pernicious

예 *a disastrous defeat*

---

unnoticed [ʌnnóutist]   주목되지 않은

뜻 not noticed

동 unheeded, unmarked, unobserved, unseen, unsighted

예 *Hoped his departure had passed unnoticed.*

---

distant [dístənt]   먼

뜻 separated in space or coming from or going to a distance

동 far, faraway, outlying, remote, removed

예 *distant villages*

---

reliance [rilàiəns]   신뢰, 의지

뜻 certainty based on past experience

동 belief, confidence, dependence, faith, trust

예 *He put more reliance in his own two legs than in the gun.*

---

trade [treid]   직업

뜻 the skilled practice of a practical occupation

동 business, craft, metier, occupation, profession

예 *He learned his trade as an apprentice.*

---

radical [rǽdikəl]   근본적인

뜻 very important and great in degree

동 basal, cardinal, fundamental, primary, vital

예 *radical leaves*

specific [spisifik]　　　　　　　　　　　　명확한

图 applying to or characterized by or distinguishing something particular or special or unique

동 authentic, definite, explicit, precise, unambiguous

예 *a specific and detailed account of the accident*

scream [skrí:m]　　　　　　　　　　　　소리치다

图 utter a sudden loud cry

동 bellow, shout, shrill, squeal, yell

예 *I screamed to her from the window but she couldn't hear me.*

graduate [grǽdʒuèit]　　　　　　　　　　졸업하다

图 confer an academic degree upon

동 certify, earn, finish, grant diploma, take a degree

예 *This school graduates 2,000 students each year.*

concrete [kánkri:t]　　　　　　　　　　구체적인

图 capable of being perceived by the senses not abstract or imaginary

동 actual, real, sensible, specific, tangible

예 *concrete objects such as trees*

impressive [impresiv]　　　　　　강한 인상을 주는

图 producing a strong effect

동 effective, imposing, influential, striking, vital

예 *gave an impressive performance as Othello*

descend [disénd]　　　　　　　　　　내려가다

图 move downward and lower, but not necessarily all the way

동 alight, drop, fall, sink, subside

예 *The curtain descend on the diva.*

reliant [riláiənt]   신뢰하는

图 relying on another for support

图 confident, contingent, dependent, liable, trustful

예 *reliant on Middle Eastern oil*

---

research [risɛ́ːrtʃ]   조사하다

图 inquire into

图 examine, explore, inquire, investigate, search

예 *He researched for information on his relatives on the web.*

---

distribution [dìstrəbjúːʃən]   분배

图 the spatial or geographic property of being scattered about over a range, area, or volume

图 allocation, apportionment, dispensation, division, partition

예 *worldwide in distribution*

---

appropriate [əprouprieit]   적당한

图 suitable for a particular person or place or condition etc.

图 applicable, felicitous, opportune, congruous, apt

예 *a book not appropriate for children*

---

specialize [speʃəlaiz]   전문화하다, 특수화하다

图 become more focus on an area of activity or field of study

图 specify, differentiate, particularize

예 *She specializes in Near Eastern history.*

---

improve [impruːv]   개선하다

图 to make better

图 amend, ameliorate, better, meliorate, refine

예 *The editor improved the manuscript with his changes.*

suck [sʌk]   빨다

圐 draw into the mouth by creating a practical vacuum in the mouth

圐 absorb, engulf, extract, imbibe, suction

圙 *suck on a straw*

drastic [drǽstik]   격렬한

圐 forceful and extreme and rigorous

圐 extreme, forceful, immoderate, radical, severe

圙 *drastic measures*

seek [síːk]   추구하다

圐 make an effort or attempt

圐 aim, attempt, endeavor, strive, try

圙 *She always seeks to do good in the world.*

habit [hǽbit]   습관

圐 an automatic pattern of behavior in reaction to a specific situation

圐 bias, constitution, disposition, mannerism, propensity

圙 *She had a habit twirling the ends of her hair.*

revolution [rèvəlúːʃən]   혁명

圐 a drastic and far-reaching change in ways of thinking and behaving

圐 innovation, mutiny, rebellion, reformation, uproar

圙 *The industrial revolution was also a cultural revolution.*

alienation [èiljənéiʃən]   소외감

圐 the feeling of being alienated from other people

圐 disaffection, estrangement, indifference, rupture, separation

圙 *His behavior alienated the other students.*

mature [mətjúər]   성숙한

医 fully developed or matured and ready to be eaten or used

동 grown, matured, mellow, ripened, sophisticated

예 *full-bodied mature wines*

---

defect [di:fekt]   결점

医 an imperfection in an object or machine

동 deficiency, demerit, failure, imperfection, shortcoming

예 *A defect caused the crystal to shatter.*

---

gather [gǽðər]   모으다, 그러모으다

医 assemble or get together

동 garner, collect, unite, convene, amass

예 *gather some stones*

---

package [pǽkidʒ]   꾸러미

医 a collection of things wrapped or boxed together

동 bale, bundle, packet, packing, parcel

예 *software package*

---

observance [əbzɑ:rvəns]   준수

医 conformity with law or custom or practice etc

동 awareness, cognizance, fidelity, keeping, obedience

예 *a religious observance*

---

abandon [əbǽndən]   버리다

医 stop maintaining or insisting on

동 forsake, leave, quit, relinquish, renounce

예 *He abandoned the thought of asking for her hand in marriage.*

significance [signífikəns]   중요

图 the quality of being significant

图 authority, importance, influence, magnitude, weightiness

예 *Do not underestimate the significance of nuclear power.*

panic [pǽnik]   공포, 공황

图 sudden mass fear and anxiety over anticipated events

图 affright, alarm, fright, scare, terror

예 *panic in the stock market*

consequence [kánsəkwens]   결과

图 a phenomenon that follows and is caused by some previous phenomenon

图 effect, event, outcome, result, upshot

예 *He acted very wise after the consequence.*

develop [diveləp]   발달시키다

图 make something new, such as a product or a mental or artistic creation

图 advance, expand, evolve, flourish, promote

예 *They developed a new technique.*

complicated [kámpləkeitid]   복잡한

图 difficult to analyze or understand

图 difficult, complex, involved, labyrinthine, mixed

예 *a complicated problem*

huge [hju:dʒ]   거대한

图 unusually great in size or amount or degree or especially extent or scope

图 enormous, immense, mighty, tremendous, vast

예 *huge numbers of birds*

grab [grǽb]   움켜쥐다

图 take hold of so as to seize or restrain or stop the motion of;

图 catch, clutch, grasp, seize, take

예 *Grab the elevator door!*

---

industry [indəstri]   근면, 성실

图 persevering determination to perform a task

图 assiduity, dedication, diligence, industriousness, sedulity

예 *His industry won him quick promotions.*

---

*Vocabulary/Expressions

Day 14

qualified [kwάləfàid]   적임의
- 뜻 meeting the proper standards and requirements and training for an office or position or task
- 동 able, competent, fit, skilled, trained
- 예 *many qualified applicants for the job*

reply [riplài]   대답하다
- 뜻 react verbally
- 동 answer, echo, feedback, react, respond
- 예 *She didn't want to reply.*

blank [blæ̀ŋk]   빈
- 뜻 any void space
- 동 empty, hollow, vacant, vacuous, void
- 예 *a blank space*

roughly [rʌfli]   대략
- 뜻 imprecise but fairly close to correct
- 동 about, approximately, around, practically, pretty near
- 예 *lasted roughly an hour*

diligent [dílədʒənt]   근면한
- 뜻 characterized by care and perseverance in carrying out tasks
- 동 assiduous, hardworking, industrious, laborious, sedulous
- 예 *a diligent search of the files*

crush [krʌʃ]   눌러 부수다
- 뜻 to compress with violence, out of natural shape or condition
- 동 grind, mash, press, squash, squeeze
- 예 *Crush an aluminum can.*

boundary [bàundəri] 경계

图 the line or plane indicating the limit or extent of something

동 ambit, border, frontier, limit, verge

예 *fishing boundary*

conceal [kənsí:l] 숨기다

图 prevent from being seen or discovered

동 bury, cover, dissemble, hide, veil

예 *Muslim women conceal their faces.*

pine [pàin] 애타게 그리워하다

图 have a desire for something or someone who is not present

동 agonize, languish, long, mourn, yearn

예 *I am pining for my lover.*

elegant [éligənt] 우아한

图 refined and tasteful in appearance or behavior or style

동 dainty, graceful, neat, refined, stylish

예 *elegant handwriting*

presentation [pri:zenteiʃən] 발표

图 a show or display

동 announcement, exhibition, exposition, manifestation, publication

예 *the presentation of new data*

rare [réər] 드문

图 marked by an uncommon quality

동 exceptional, infrequent, sparse, uncommon, unusual

예 *She was kind to an rare degree.*

brilliant [bríljənt]   훌륭한

图 having or marked by unusual and impressive intelligence

图 effulgent, luminous, lustrous, shining, splendid

예 *a brilliant solution to the problem*

irritated [írəteitid]   신경질이 난

图 aroused to impatience or anger

图 annoyed, miffed, peeved, riled, roiled

예 *made an irritated gesture*

stock [sták]   들여놓다

图 amass so as to keep for future use or sale or for a particular occasion or use

图 accumulate, furnish, provide, store, supply

예 *Let's stock coffee as long as prices are low.*

respect [rispekt]   존경하다

图 to regard with special attention

图 esteem, honor, regard, revere, venerate

예 *respect your parents!*

introduce [intrədju:s]   소개하다

图 cause to come to know personally

图 acquaint, announce, familiarize, present, suggest

예 *introduce the new neighbors to the community*

essence [ésns]   본질

图 the choicest or most essential or most vital part of some idea or experience

图 core, gist, pith, significance, substance

예 *the essence of the prosecutor's argument*

fear [fíər]   무서움

图 an emotion experienced in anticipation of some specific pain or danger

图 alarm, dread, fright, scare, terror

예 *the fear of God*

---

survey [sərvei]   조사하다

图 look over carefully or inspect

图 check, examine, inspect, research, scrutinize

예 *He surveyed his new classmates.*

---

strength [streŋkθ]   강점, 장점

图 an asset of special worth or utility

图 strong point, advantage, speciality, forte, metier

예 *Cooking is his strength.*

---

fare [fέər]   운임

图 the sum charged for riding in a public conveyance

图 charge, expense, price, ticket, toll

예 *a taxi fare*

---

persuade [pərswéid]   설득하다

图 cause somebody to adopt a certain position, belief, or course of action

图 argue, coax, convince, induce, prevail

예 *You can't persuade me to buy this ugly vase.*

---

serious [síəriəs]   진지한

图 concerned with work or important matters rather than play or trivialities

图 deliberate, earnest, pensive, solemn, staid

예 *Are you serious or joking?*

modify [mɑ́dəfai]   변경하다, 수정하다

图 cause to change

图 alter, adapt, correct, transform, revise

예 *The discussion has modified my thinking about the issue*

fortunately [fɔ́:rt ʃ ənətli]   다행히

图 by good fortune

图 auspiciously, favorably, luckily, happily, swimmingly

예 *Fortunately the weather was good.*

conflict [kɑ́nflikt]   투쟁

图 an open clash between two opposing groups or individuals

图 battle, contest, fight, struggle, warfare

예 *The harder the conflict the more glorious the triumph.*

comprehend [kὰmprihénd]   이해하다

图 get the meaning of something

图 apprehend, grasp, grok, savvy, understand

예 *Do you comprehend the meaning of this letter?*

assemble [əsémbl]   모으다

图 collect in one place

图 aggregate, forgather, gather, meet, rally

예 *We assembled in the church basement.*

outdoor [autdɔ́:r]   집 밖의, 옥외의, 야외의

图 located, suited for, or taking place in the open air

图 alfresco, outside, exterior, outer, outward, exterior

예 *outdoor clothes*

Day 14

result [rizʌlt]   결과

🔲 a phenomenon that follows and is caused by some previous phenomenon

🔲 consequence, effect, event, outcome, upshot

🔲 *The magnetic result was greater when the rod was lengthwise.*

unimaginable [ʌnimǽdʒinəbl]   상상할 수 없는

🔲 totally unlikely

🔲 impossible, improbable, inconceivable, undreamed-of, unthinkable

🔲 *previously unimaginable*

competent [kámpətənt]   유능한

🔲 properly or sufficiently qualified or capable or efficient

🔲 proficient, skilled, able, qualified, sufficient

🔲 *a competent typist*

direct [direkt]   직접적인

🔲 straightforward in means or manner or behavior or language or action

🔲 categorical, explicit, outspoken, straightforward, unreserved

🔲 *a direct question*

adjust [ədʒʌst]   조절하다

🔲 alter or regulate so as to achieve accuracy or conform to a standard

🔲 correct, fit, set, settle, tune

🔲 *Adjust the clock, please.*

feature [fiːtʃər]   특징

🔲 a prominent attribute or aspect of something

🔲 attribute, characteristic, idiosyncrasy, property, trait

🔲 *Generosity is one of his best features.*

colleague [káli:g]   동료

图 a person who is member of one's class or profession

图 associate, companion, confrere, fellow, mate

예 *The surgeon consulted his colleagues.*

---

perfection [pərfékʃən]   완전, 완벽

图 the state of being without a flaw or defect

图 completeness, faultlessness, flawlessness, improvement, paragon

예 *the acme of perfection*

---

violent [vàiələnt]   격렬한, 난폭한

图 acting with or marked by or resulting from great force or energy or emotional
intensity

图 fierce, furious, intense, severe, vehement

예 *a violent attack*

---

arise [əràiz]   일어나다

图 come into existence

图 appear, develop, emerge, originate, spring

예 *A new religious movement arose in that country.*

---

unburden [ʌnbə́ːrdn]   ~의 짐을 내려놓다

图 take the burden off

图 disburden, discharge, ease, relieve, unload

예 *unburden the donkey*

---

combine [kəmbàin]   결합시키다

图 put or add together

图 amalgamate, connect, incorporate, mix, unite

예 *combine resources*

---

pledge [pledʒ]　　　　　　　　　　　　　　　　　맹세하다

뜻 promise solemnly and formally

동 affirm, certify, confirm, promise, swear

예 *I pledge that I will honor my wife.*

misconception [miskənsepʃən]　　　　　　오해, 잘못된 생각

뜻 an incorrect conception

동 misapprehension, misunderstanding, error, fallacy, misinterpretation

예 *a serious misconception*

manufacture [mənjufǽktʃər]　　　　　　　　제조하다

뜻 put together out of artificial or natural components or parts

동 construct, fabricate, make, produce

예 *They manufacture small toys.*

complex [kəmpleks]　　　　　　　　　　　　　복잡한

뜻 a conceptual whole made up of complicated and related parts

동 complicated, elaborate, intricate, involved, knotty

예 *The complex of shopping malls, houses, and roads created a new town.*

horror [hɔ:rər]　　　　　　　　　　　　　　　공포

뜻 something that inspires dislike

동 abhorrence, dread, fear, fright, terror

예 *The painting that others found so beautiful was a horror to him.*

donate [douneit]　　　　　　　　　　　　　　기부하다

뜻 give to a charity or good cause

동 bestow, contribute, endow, grant, present

예 *donate money to the orphanage*

absence [ǽbsəns]   부재

图 the state of being absent

동 default, deficiency, lack, shortage, want

예 *He was surprised by the absence of any explanation.*

---

advance [ædvǽns]   나아가게 하다

图 contribute to the progress or growth of

동 encourage, boost, proceed, progress, promote

예 *I am advancing the use of computers in the classroom.*

---

*Vocabulary/Expressions

---

schedule [skedʒu(:)l]   예정하다
- 뜻 plan for an activity or event
- 통 appoint, book, reserve, engage, arrange
- 예 *I've scheduled a concert next week*

---

critic [kritik]   비평가
- 뜻 someone who frequently finds fault or makes harsh and unfair judgments
- 통 analyst, interpreter, connoisseur, evaluator, reviewer
- 예 *art critic*

---

accuracy [ǽkjurəsi]   정확성
- 뜻 the quality of being near to the true value
- 통 precision, correctness, preciseness, exactness, exactitude
- 예 *he was beginning to doubt the accuracy of his compass*

---

reward [riwɔ:rd]   보수
- 뜻 a recompense for worthy acts or retribution for wrongdoing
- 통 wages, payment, prize, compensation, recompense
- 예 *virtue is its own reward*

---

amaze [əmeiz]   몹시 놀라게 하다
- 뜻 affect with wonder
- 통 astonish, surprise, shock, stun, startle
- 예 *Your ability to speak six languages amazes me!*

---

servant [sɛ:rvənt]   하인
- 뜻 a person working in the service of another
- 통 retainer, slave, menial, attendant, minion
- 예 *public servant*

---

enable [ineibl]   가능하게 하다

图 render capable or able for some task

图 allow, authorize, capacitate, empower, accredit

예 *This skill will enable you to find a job on Wall Street*

longing [lɔ:ŋiŋ]   갈망, 동경

图 prolonged unfulfilled desire or need

图 yearning, desire, craving, hankering, hunger

예 *a secret longing*

exert [igzə :rt]   (힘·능력·지력 등을) 쓰다

图 put to use

图 apply, exercise, endeavor, strive, utilize

예 *exert one's power or influence*

category [kǽtəgɔ:ri]   범주

图 a collection of things sharing a common attribute

图 classification, type, class, department, sort

예 *there are two categories of detergents*

recommendation [rekəmendei ʃ ən]   추천장

图 any quality or characteristic that gains a person a favorable reception or acceptance or admission

图 reference, advice, testimonial, approbation, endorsement,

예 *her pleasant personality is already a recommendation*

stubborn [stʌbərn]   완고한, 고집센

图 tenaciously unwilling or marked by tenacious unwillingness to yield

图 obstinate, unregenerate, unyielding, tenacious, rigid

예 *a stubborn resistance*

labor [leibər]   노동

圆 productive work

圖 toil, chore, job, task

뗵 *his labor did not require a great deal of skill*

---

occasion [əkeiʒən]   경우, 때

圆 an event that occurs at a critical time

圖 juncture, incident, occurrence, happening, case

뗵 *it was needed only on special occasions*

---

significant [signifikənt]   중요한

圆 important in effect or meaning

圖 critical, notable, vital, momentous, serious

뗵 *a significant change in tax laws*

---

crooked [krukid]   구부러진

圆 not straight or aligned

圖 bent, angled, curved, devious, oblique

뗵 *crooked country roads*

---

sufficient [səfiʃənt]   충분한

圆 of a quantity that can fulfill a need or requirement but without being
abundant

圖 enough, adequate, ample, plenty, competent

뗵 *sufficient food*

---

indifferent [indifərənt]   무관심한

圆 marked by a lack of interest

圖 apathetic, uninterested, unconcerned, disinterested, nonchalant

뗵 *an indifferent audience*

researcher [risə :rt ʃ ər]   연구원, 조사자, 탐색자

圏 a scientist who devotes himself to doing research

图 investigator, explorer, researchist, experimenter, tester

예 *an independent researcher*

---

recognize [rekəgnaiz]   인정하다, 인지하다

圏 accept (someone) to be what is claimed or accept his power and authority

图 acknowledge, understand, admit, perceive, comprehend

예 *We do not recognize your gods*

---

capability [keipəbiləti]   능력

圏 the quality of being capable

图 ability,

예 *he worked to the limits of his capability*

---

thrust [θ rʌst]   밀다

圏 push forcefully

图 advance, press, plunge, shove, poke

예 *He thrust his chin forward*

---

blueprint [blu:print]   청사진

圏 something intended as a guide for making something else

图 design, pattern, plan, layout, scheme

예 *a blueprint for a house*

---

gaze [geiz]   응시하다

圏 look at with fixed eyes

图 stare, contemplate, peer, scrutinize, inspect

예 *The students stared at the teacher with amazement*

---

unconscious [ʌnkánʃəs]　　　　　　　　　　　모르는, 알아채지 못하는

- 뜻 not knowing or perceiving
- 동 ignorant, senseless, insensible, unaware, unwitting
- 예 *happily unconscious of the new calamity at home*

flip [flip]　　　　　　　　　　　　　　　　　　　　튀기다

- 뜻 lightly throw to see which side comes up
- 동 toss, throw, flick, cast, fillip
- 예 *I don't know what to do--I may as well flip a coin!*

stimulate [stimjuleit]　　　　　　　　　　　　　자극하다

- 뜻 act as a stimulant
- 동 excite, provoke, incite, galvanize, rouse
- 예 *The book stimulated her imagination*

thump [θʌmp]　　　　　　　　　　　　　　　　　탁 치다

- 뜻 make a dull sound
- 동 thud, hit, bang, beat, punch
- 예 *the knocker thumped against the front door*

social [souʃəl]　　　　　　　　　　　　　사회적인, 사회의

- 뜻 relating to human society and its members
- 동 public, communal, gregarious, societal
- 예 *social institutions*

prevalence [prevələns]　　　　　　　　　　　　　　유행

- 뜻 being widespread
- 동 currency, popularity, vogue, pervasiveness
- 예 *he was surprised by the prevalence of optimism about the future*

neutral [njuːtrəl]　　　　　　　　　　　　　　　　　중립의

图 having no personal preference

图 impartial, neuter, indifferent, unbiased, unprejudiced

예 *a neutral observer*

---

ignorance [ignərəns]　　　　　　　　　　　　　　　무지

图 the lack of knowledge or education

图 nescience, darkness, blindness, unawareness, simplicity

예 *Ignorance is bliss*

---

contaminate [kəntǽməneit]　　　　　　　　　　오염시키다

图 make impure

图 pollute, stain, taint, vitiate, infect

예 *The industrial wastes contaminated the lake*

---

overbearing [ouvərbɛ̀əriŋ]　　　　　　　　　건방진, 거만한

图 having or showing arrogant superiority to and disdain of those one views as unworthy

图 disdainful, haughty, imperious, lordly, prideful

예 *walked with a overbearing swagger*

---

assembly [əsembli]　　　　　　　　　　　　　　집회, 집합

图 a group of persons who are gathered together for a common purpose

图 congregation, assemblage, cluster, crowd, gathering

예 *they demanded the right of assembly*

---

unusual [ʌnjuːʒuəl]　　　　　　　　　　비범한, 보기 드문

图 not usual or common or ordinary

图 extraordinary, distinguished, remarkable, uncommon, unique

예 *a man of unusual ability*

value [vǽlju:]   가치

뜻 the quality (positive or negative) that renders something desirable or valuable

동 worth, merit, meaning, usefulness

예 *the Shakespearean Shylock is of dubious value in the modern world*

---

globe [gloub]   지구

뜻 the planet we live on

동 earth, world, ball

예 *the globe moves around the sun*

---

agency [eidʒənsi]   대리, 대행

뜻 the state of serving as an official and authorized delegate or agent

동 instrumentality, intercession, intervention, medium

예 *advertising agency*

---

refine [ri:fain]   정제하다

뜻 reduce to a fine, unmixed, or pure state

동 purify, rarefy, clarify, cleanse, filter

예 *refine sugar*

---

automatic [ɔ:təmǽtik]   자동의

뜻 operating with minimal human intervention

동 mechanical, reflex, self-acting, self-moving, perfunctory

예 *automatic transmission*

---

rumor [ru:mər]   소문

뜻 gossip (usually a mixture of truth and untruth) passed around by word of mouth

동 hearsay, whisper, talk, bruit, canard

예 *rumor mill*

---

qualify [kwálǝfai]   ...에게 자격을 주다

図 make fit or prepared

됨 authorize, empower, entitle, sanction, commission

예 *Your education qualifies you for this job*

---

strategy [strǽtǝdʒi]   전략

図 an elaborate and systematic plan of action

됨 strategics, tactics, stratagem

예 *marketing strategy*

---

level [levǝl]   동일수준

図 a position on a scale of intensity or amount or quality

됨 degree, grade, rank, stage, standard

예 *a high level of care is required*

---

recently [ri:sntli]   최근에

図 in the recent past

됨 late, lately, currently, newly, afresh

예 *he was in Paris recently*

---

arrive [ǝraiv]   도착하다

図 reach a destination

됨 come, get, show up

예 *She arrived home at 7 o'clock*

---

knowledge [nálidʒ]   지식

図 the psychological result of perception and learning and reasoning

됨 cognition, intelligence, information, scholarship, learning

예 *domain knowledge*

---

rank [rǽŋk]   계급, 계층

㈜ relative status

㈜ hierarchy, level, class, degree, grade

㈜ *his salary was determined by his rank and seniority*

---

involve [inválv]   포함하다

㈜ contain as a part

㈜ include, contain, comprise, incorporate, imply

㈜ *Dinner at Joe's always involves at least six courses*

---

*Vocabulary/Expressions

Day 16

draw [drɔ:]   당기다, 끌다

㈜ cause to move by pulling

㈱ attract, drag, draft, haul, trail,

㈖ *draw a wagon*

---

striking [straikiŋ]   현저한, 두드러진

㈜ having a quality that thrusts itself into attention

㈱ outstanding, prominent, salient, spectacular, remarkable

㈖ *a striking resemblance between parent and child*

---

float [flout]   뜨다

㈜ be in motion due to some air or water current

㈱ drift,   be adrift, blow

㈖ *The leaves were floating in the wind*

---

expressive [ikspresiv]   표현적인

㈜ characterized by expression

㈱ revealing, telling, indicative, expressional

㈖ *a very expressive face*

---

soar [sɔ:r]   높이 치솟다

㈜ rise rapidly

㈱ surge, lift, arise, shoot up

㈖ *the dollar soared against the yen*

---

influential [influen ʃ əl]   영향력이 있는

㈜ having or exercising influence or power

㈱ powerful, dominant, leading, prominent, authoritative

㈖ *an influential newspaper*

---

reliable [rilaiəbl]   믿을 수 있는, 의지가 되는

뜻 worthy of reliance or trust

동 dependable, trustworthy, faithful, certain, veracious

예 *a reliable source of information*

---

particular [pərtikjulər]   특별한

뜻 unique or specific to a person or thing or category

동 peculiar, special, uncommon, marked, notable

예 *the particular demands of the job*

---

zeal [zi:l]   열심

뜻 a feeling of strong eagerness

동 ardor, elan, enthusiasm, zest, passion

예 *He felt a kind of religious zeal.*

---

suspend [səspend]   일시 중지하다

뜻 stop a process or a habit by imposing a freeze on it

동 discontinue, pause, cease, abandon, abort

예 *Suspend the aid to the war-torn country*

---

relate [rileit]   관련시키다

뜻 make a logical or causal connection

동 associate, link, colligate, connect, pertain

예 *I cannot relate these events at all*

---

elaborate [ilǽbərət]   정교한, 복잡한

뜻 developed or executed with care and in minute detail

동 detailed, sophisticated, precise, complicated, complex

예 *the elaborate register of the inhabitants prevented tax evasion*

registration [redʒistrei ʃ ən]   등록, 기재

图 the act of enrolling

동 enrollment, listing, recording, registry, entry

예 *resident registration*

---

welfare [welfɛ̀ər]   복지

图 governmental provision of economic assistance to persons in need

동 well-being, prosperity, weal, good, public assistance

예 *she lives on welfare*

---

position [pəzi ʃ ən]   위치

图 the particular portion of space occupied by something

동 place, site, location, space, spot

예 *he put the lamp back in its position*

---

possibility [pàsəbiləti]   가능성

图 capability of existing or happening or being true

동 feasibility, likelihood, probability, prospect, potential

예 *there is a possibility that his sense of smell has been impaired*

---

mysterious [mistiəriəs]   신비한, 불가사의한

图 of an obscure nature

동 inscrutable, mystifying, weird, occult, strange

예 *in its mysterious past it encompasses all the dim origins of life- Rachel Carson*

---

solitude [sάlətju:d]   고독

图 a state of social isolation

동 aloneness, loneliness, isolation, desolation, solitariness

예 *He liked solitude*

---

frustrate [frʌstreit]   좌절시키다

图 hinder or prevent (the efforts, plans, or desires) of

图 thwart, disappoint, discourage, dishearten, obstruct

예 *What ultimately frustrated every challenger was Ruth's amazing September surge*

sympathetic [simpəθetik]   동정심 있는, 인정 있는

图 showing or motivated by sympathy and understanding and generosity

图 charitable, benevolent, kindly, openhearted, considerate

예 *a sympathetic act*

revolutionize [revəlu:ʃənaiz]   혁명을 일으키다, 급격한 변화를 가져오다

图 change radically

图 overturn, transform, reform, recast, refashion

예 *E-mail revolutionized communication in academe*

unintended [ʌnintendid]   고의가 아닌

图 not deliberate

图 unintentional, involuntary, unwitting, undesigned, accidental

예 *unintended effect*

contribute [kəntribju:t]   기여하다

图 be conducive to

图 conduce, present, grant, proffer, dispense

예 *The use of computers in the classroom contribute to better writing*

dictator [dikteitər]   독재자, 절대 권력자

图 a ruler who is unconstrained by law

图 potentate, absolutist, authoritarian, despot, tyrant

예 *a cruel dictator*

modify [mάdəfai]　　　　　　　　　　　　　　　　변경하다, 수정하다

뜻 cause to change

동 alter, adapt, correct, transform, revise

예 *The discussion has modified my thinking about the issue*

---

degree [digri:]　　　　　　　　　　　　　　　　　　정도, 등급

뜻 a position on a scale of intensity or amount or quality

동 grade, level, rank, stage, standard

예 *it is all a matter of degree*

---

frequent [fri:kwənt]　　　　　　　　　　　　　　　　빈번한

뜻 coming at short intervals or habitually

동 common, repeated, continual, reiterative, constant

예 *frequent complaints*

---

possess [pəzes]　　　　　　　　　　　　　　　　　소유하다

뜻 have ownership or possession of

동 own, have, obtain, hold, retain

예 *We possess three houses in Florida*

---

produce [prədju:s]　　　　　　　　　　　　　　　　생산하다

뜻 create or manufacture a man-made product

동 develop, engender, generate, make, manufacture

예 *We produce more cars than we can sell*

---

devise [divaiz]　　　　　　　　　　　　　　　　방법을 고안하다

뜻 come up with an idea, plan, explanation, theory, or principle after a mental effort

동 invent, contrive, excogitate, formulate, conceive

예 *excogitate a way to measure the speed of light*

---

greed [gri:d]　　　　　　　　　　탐욕
图 insatiable desire for wealth
图 avarice, covetousness, rapacity, cupidity, voracity
예 *greed for food*

bounce [bauns]　　　　　　　　　튀다
图 spring back
图 resile, bound, rebound, recoil, reverberate
예 *The rubber ball bounced*

thrive [θraiv]　　　　　　　　　번영하다
图 grow vigorously
图 blossom, flourish, grow, succeed, prosper
예 *The deer population in this town is thriving*

organize [ɔ:rgənaiz]　　　　　　조직하다
图 create as an entity
图 form, systematize, arrange, construct, formulate
예 *They organized a company*

considerable [kənsidərəbl]　　　상당한
图 large or relatively large in number or amount or extent or degree
图 important, notable, significant, sizable, substantial
예 *spent a considerable amount of time on the problem*

punctual [pʌŋktʃuəl]　　　시간을 잘 지키는
图 acting or arriving or performed exactly at the time appointed
图 timely, seasonable, appropriate, fitting, opportune
예 *she expected guests to be punctual at meals*

healthy [helθi]   건강한, 건전한

뜻 having or indicating good health in body or mind

동 sound, wholesome, healthful, salutary, hale

예 *a rosy healthy baby*

---

spectator [spekteitər]   구경꾼

뜻 someone who looks at something

동 onlooker, bystander, beholder, observer, watcher

예 *the spectators applauded the performance*

---

discomfort [diskʌmfərt]   불쾌, 불안

뜻 an uncomfortable feeling of mental painfulness or distress

동 uncomfortableness, soreness, irritation, uneasiness, malaise

예 *discomfort index*

---

establish [istæbliʃ]   설립하다

뜻 set up or found

동 organize, institute, settle, constitute, base

예 *She establish a literacy program*

---

trim [trim]   다듬다, 정돈하다

뜻 remove the edges from and cut down to the desired size

동 pare, curtail, edit, lop, snip

예 *trim the photograph*

---

storage [stɔːridʒ]   저장

뜻 a depository for goods

동 storehouse, entrepot, store, ambry, stockpile

예 *storages were built close to the docks*

pure [pjuər]   순수한

围 free of extraneous elements of any kind

동 unmixed, clean, immaculate, chaste, clear

예 *pure air and water*

---

evaluation [ivæljuei ∫ ən]   평가

围 an appraisal of the value of something

동 valuation, rating, appraisement, assessment, estimation

예 *he set a high evaluation on friendship*

---

offer [ɔ:fər]   제공하다, 제출하다

围 present for acceptance or rejection

동 proffer, provide, submit, give, propose,

예 *She offered us all a cold drink*

---

leisure [li:ʒər]   여가

围 freedom to choose a pastime or enjoyable activity

동 rest, recreation, vacation, holiday, liberty

예 *he lacked the leisure for golf*

---

inspire [inspaiər]   고무하다, 격려하다

围 heighten or intensify

동 invigorate, enliven, exalt, encourage, stimulate

예 *These paintings inspire the imagination*

---

introduction [intrədʌk ∫ ən]   도입, 창시

围 the act of starting something for the first time

동 initiation, foundation, institution, origination, instauration

예 *she looked forward to her introduction as an adult*

---

therefore [ðὲərfɔːr]　　　　　　　　　　　　　　　그러므로

图 (used to introduce a logical conclusion) from that fact or reason or as a result

图 hence, thence, thus, so

例 *therefore X must be true*

---

doom [duːm]　　　　　　　　　　　　　　　　　　운명, 파멸

图 an unpleasant or disastrous destiny

图 doomsday, fate, catastrophe, destination, disaster

例 *everyone was aware of the approaching doom but was helpless to avoid it*

---

*Vocabulary/Expressions

Day 17

enrollment [inroulmənt]   등록, 기재

뜻 the act of enrolling

통 registration, listing, recording, registry, entry

예 *school enrollment*

---

occur [əkɛ :r]   일어나다

뜻 come to pass

통 happen, take place, befall, ensue, transpire

예 *Nothing occurred that seemed important*

---

ordinary [ɔ:rdəneri]   평상의, 보통의

뜻 not exceptional in any way especially in quality or ability or size or degree

통 common, regular, normal, typical, usual

예 *ordinary everyday objects*

---

landfill [lǽndfil]   매립지

뜻 a low area that has been filled in

통 dump, disposal area, junkyard, rubbish pile, recycling station

예 *landfill tax*

---

irresistible [irizistəbl]   저항할 수 없는

뜻 impossible to resist

통 resistless, overpowering, resistless, compelling, overwhelming

예 *irresistible impulses*

---

density [densəti]   밀도

뜻 the amount per unit size

통 concentration, tightness, compactness, consistency, denseness

예 *high density*

---

achieve [ətʃiːv]   이루다, 성취하다

뜻 to gain with effort

동 accomplish, attain, reach, perform, obtain

예 *she achieved her goal despite setbacks*

---

artificial [à:rtəfiʃəl]   인조의, 인공적인

뜻 contrived by art rather than nature

동 factitious, false, unnatural, unreal, man-made

예 *artificial flavoring*

---

disassemble [disəsembl]   해체하다, 분해하다

뜻 take apart into its constituent pieces

동 dismantle, demount, dismount, take apart

예 *disassemble a computer*

---

oval [ouvəl]   달걀 모양의, 타원형의

뜻 rounded like an egg

동 elliptic, elliptical, ovate, oviform, ovoid

예 *oval shape*

---

beverage [bevəridʒ]   마실 것, 음료

뜻 any liquid suitable for drinking

동 drink, drinkable, potable, brew, cooler

예 *may I take your beverage order?*

---

digest [didʒest]   소화하다

뜻 convert food into absorbable substances

동 assimilate, absorb, dissolve, break down

예 *I cannot digest milk products*

symptom [simptəm]   징후, 징조

图 any sensation or change in bodily function that is experienced by a patient and is associated with a particular disease

图 sign, indication, mark, token, indicia

예 *withdrawal symptom*

---

architect [á:rkətekt]   건축가, 설계자

图 someone who creates plans to be used in making something

图 designer, builder, creator, draftsperson, maker

예 *creative architect*

---

object [ábdʒikt]   물체

图 a tangible and visible entity

图 body, item, thing, subject, matter

예 *it was full of rackets, balls and other objects*

---

recall [rikɔ:l]   상기하다

图 recall knowledge from memory

图 remember, retrieve, recollect, reminisce, retrospect

예 *Do you recall that he once loved you?*

---

root [ru:t]   근원

图 the place where something begins, where it springs into being

图 beginning, origin, rootage, source, base

예 *communism's Russian root*

---

delay [dilei]   늦추다

图 cause to be slowed down or delayed

图 detain, defer, postpone, procrastinate, adjourn

예 *Traffic was delayed by the bad weather*

---

tiny [taini]   작은

图 very small

图 diminutive, lilliputian, midget, petite, minute

예 *tiny feet*

---

wisdom [wizdəm]   지혜

图 accumulated knowledge or erudition or enlightenment

图 sapience, intelligence, learning, insight, perspicacity

예 *Wisdom literature*

---

editorial [edətɔːriəl]   사설

图 an article giving opinions or perspectives

图 column, commentary, article, critique, review

예 *an editorial about politics*

---

bridge [bridʒ]   교량 역할을 하는 것, 중개

图 something resembling a bridge in form or function

图 connection, bond, link, tie

예 *his letters provided a bridge across the centuries*

---

specialty [spe ʃ əlti]   전문, 장기, 전공

图 an asset of special worth or utility

图 forte, strength, metier, major, peculiarity

예 *cooking is his specialty*

---

protection [prətek ʃ ən]   보호

图 the activity of protecting someone or something

图 care, guardianship, safeguard, security, shield

예 *the witnesses demanded police protection*

confine [kənfain]   한정하다, 제한하다

- 図 place limits on
- 图 restrict, restrain, trammel, immure, constrain
- 예 *confine the use of this parking lot*

competition [kàmpəti ʃ ən]   경쟁

- 図 the act of competing as for profit or a prize
- 图 contention, rivalry, contest, emulation, match
- 예 *the teams were in fierce competition for first place*

equate [ikweit]   동등하다고 생각하다

- 図 consider or describe as similar, equal, or analogous
- 图 compare, liken, balance, equalize, even
- 예 *You cannot equate success in financial matters with greed*

sharp [ʃ ά:rp]   날카로운, 예리한

- 図 having or demonstrating ability to recognize or draw fine distinctions
- 图 acute, discriminating, incisive, keen, piercing
- 예 *as sharp and incisive as the stroke of a fang*

nationwide [nei ʃ ənwaid]   전국적인

- 図 occurring or extending throughout a country or nation
- 图 countrywide, national, domestic, inland, public
- 예 *the event aroused nationwide interest*

share [ʃ ɛ̀ər]   몫, 할당몫, 일부분

- 図 assets belonging to or due to or contributed by an individual person or group
- 图 portion, part, allotment, percentage, dividened
- 예 *he wanted his share in cash*

exit [egzit]   출구

- 뜻 an opening that permits escape or release
- 동 issue, outlet, way out, egress,
- 예 *he blocked the exit*

ambiguous [æmbigjuəs]   모호한

- 뜻 open to two or more interpretations
- 동 equivocal, indeterminate, uncertain, unclear, vague
- 예 *an ambiguous statement*

misconception [miskənsep ʃ ən]   오해, 잘못된 생각

- 뜻 an incorrect conception
- 동 misapprehension, misunderstanding, error, fallacy, misinterpretation
- 예 *a serious misconception*

succeed [səksi:d]   성공하다

- 뜻 attain success or reach a desired goal
- 동 prosper, follow, inherit, achieve, thrive
- 예 *The enterprise succeeded*

extreme [ikstri:m]   극도의

- 뜻 of the greatest possible degree or extent or intensity
- 동 utmost, supreme, ultimate, ultra, excessive
- 예 *extreme cold*

effortless [efərtlis]   노력하지 않는, 쉬운

- 뜻 requiring or apparently requiring no effort
- 동 easy, facile, simple, undemanding, offhand
- 예 *the swallows glided in an effortless way through the busy air*

convince [kənvins]   확신시키다

图 make someone agree, understand, or realize the truth or validity of something

图 persuade, satisfy, assure, induce, demonstrate

예 *He had finally convinced several customers of the advantages of his product*

shelter [ʃeltər]   피난처

图 a structure that provides privacy and protection from danger

图 refuge, tower, asylum, haven, harbour

예 *nuclear shelter*

ally [əlai]   동맹

图 an associate who provides cooperation or assistance

图 confederate, associate, friend, accomplice, colleague

예 *he's a good ally in fight*

dip [dip]   담그다

图 immerse briefly into a liquid so as to wet, coat, or saturate

图 sink, plunge, submerge, dive, dunk

예 *dip the garment into the cleaning solution*

practical [præktikəl]   실용적인

图 guided by practical experience and observation rather than theory

图 hardheaded, pragmatic, useful, utilitarian, rational

예 *completely practical in his approach to business*

correspondence [kɔːrəspándəns]   일치, 조화

图 compatibility of observations

图 agreement, accord, coherence, coincidence, concurrence

예 *the results of two tests were in correspondence*

drop [dráp]　　　　　떨어뜨리다
- 뜻 let fall to the ground
- 동 lower, drip, sink, dribble, trickle
- 예 *Don't drop the dishes*

last [lǽst]　　　　　지속하다
- 뜻 persist for a specified period of time
- 동 endure, continue, keep on, hold, maintain
- 예 *The bad weather lasted for three days*

hurt [hə:rt]　　　　　다치게 하다
- 뜻 give trouble or pain to
- 동 blemish, injure, impair, damage, mar
- 예 *This exercise will hurt your back*

especially [ispeʃəli]　　　　　특히
- 뜻 to a distinctly greater extent or degree than is common
- 동 particularly, peculiarly, specially, notably, chiefly
- 예 *an especially cautious approach to the danger*

admit [ædmit]　　　　　인정하다
- 뜻 declare to be true or admit the existence or reality or truth of
- 동 acknowledge, accept, recognize, concede, permit
- 예 *He admitted his errors*

contest [kántest]　　　　　경쟁
- 뜻 an occasion on which a winner is selected from among two or more contestants
- 동 competition, challenge, game, match, concours
- 예 *beauty contest*

description [diskrip ∫ən]   기술, 서술

图 a statement that represents something in words

图 portrayal, representation, explanation, narrative, report

예 *job description*

---

glitter [glitər]   반짝반짝 빛나다

图 be shiny, as if wet

图 glisten, gleam, shine, sparkle, twinkle

예 *His eyes were glistening*

---

*Vocabulary/Expressions

seem [si:m]　　　　　　　　　　　　　　　　　...처럼 보이다

- 뜻 give a certain impression or have a certain outward aspect
- 동 look, appear, sound, show
- 예 *She seems to be sleeping*

---

indirect [indərekt]　　　　　　　　　　　　　　　간접적인

- 뜻 having intervening factors or persons or influences
- 동 circuitous, secondary, ambiguous, ancillary
- 예 *reflection from the ceiling provided a soft indirect light*

---

hostile [hástl]　　　　　　　　　　　　적의 있는, 적대하는

- 뜻 characterized by enmity or ill will
- 동 antagonistic, adverse, bellicose, unfriendly, unfavorable
- 예 *a hostile nation*

---

magnify [mǽgnəfai]　　　　　　　　　　　　　　확대하다

- 뜻 increase in size, volume or significance
- 동 amplify, enlarge, intensify, aggrandize, increase
- 예 *Her terror was magnified in her mind*

---

pause [pɔ:z]　　　　　　　　　　　　　　　　　　중지

- 뜻 a time interval during which there is a temporary cessation of something
- 동 intermission, break, interruption, suspension, stop
- 예 *pause button*

---

symbolic [simbálik]　　　　　　　　　　　　　　상징적인

- 뜻 relating to or using or proceeding by means of symbols
- 동 emblematic, figurative, token, characteristic, significant
- 예 *symbolic logic*

unexpected [ʌnikspektid]　　　　　　　　　　　　예기치 않은

医 not expected or anticipated

图 surprising, abrupt, unforeseen, unpredictable, fortuitous

예 *unexpected guests*

---

solitude [sάlətjuːd]　　　　　　　　　　　　　고독

医 a state of social isolation

图 aloneness, loneliness, isolation, solitariness, desolation

예 *she likes solitude*

---

intense [intens]　　　　　　　　　　　　　강렬한

医 possessing or displaying a distinctive feature to a heightened degree

图 forceful, severe, energetic, powerful, violent

예 *intense heat*

---

market [mάːrkit]　　　　　　　　　　　　　시장

医 the world of commercial activity where goods and services are bought and sold

图 mart, bazaar, trade, fair, outlet

예 *without competition there would be no market*

---

accuse [əkjuːz]　　　　　　　　　　　　　고발하다

医 bring an accusation against

图 impeach, incriminate, criminate, inculpate, denounce

예 *The neighbors accused the man of spousal abuse*

---

roll [roul]　　　　　　　　　　　　　구르다

医 move by turning over or rotating

图 turn over, wheel, trundle, revolve

예 *The child rolled down the hill*

infant [infənt] 유아

图 a very young child (birth to 1 year) who has not yet begun to walk or talk

통 baby, toddler, kid, babe, newborn

예 *she held the infant in her arms*

---

intelligent [inteləd3ənt] 지적인

图 having the capacity for thought and reason especially to a high degree

통 smart, knowledgeable, enlightened, astute, ingenious

예 *is there intelligent life in the universe?*

---

insult [insʌlt] 모욕하다

图 treat, mention, or speak to rudely

통 diss, affront, ridicule, humiliate, mock

예 *He insulted her with his rude remarks*

---

detail [diːteil] 세부, 항목

图 a small part that can be considered separately from the whole

통 particular, item, component, element, factor

예 *it was perfect in all details*

---

penetrate [penətreit] 꿰뚫다

图 pass into or through, often by overcoming resistance

통 perforate, pierce, force, bore, drill

예 *The bullet penetrated her chest*

---

challenge [t ʃ ǽlind3] 도전

图 a demanding or stimulating situation

통 dare, defiance, provocation, defy

예 *they reacted irrationally to the challenge of Russian power*

---

heart [háːrt]   감정, 심정

图 an inclination or tendency of a certain kind

图 spirit, feeling, sentiment, soul, character

예 *he had a change of heart*

meaning [míːniŋ]   의미

图 the message that is intended or expressed or signified

图 significance, signification, import, purport, definition

예 *what is the meaning of this sentence*

interrelate [intərrileit]   상호 관계를 가지다

图 be in a relationship with

图 relate, correlate, pertain, associate, concern

예 *How are these two observations interrelated*

depression [dipreʃən]   우울

图 a mental state characterized by a pessimistic sense of inadequacy and a despondent lack of activity

图 despair, desolation, gloom, melancholy, abjectness

예 *manic depression*

view [vjuː]   관점

图 a personal belief or judgment that is not founded on proof or certainty

图 opinion, sentiment, persuasion, thought, perspective

예 *my view differs from yours*

mass [mǽs]   큰 덩어리

图 a body of matter without definite shape

图 block, bunch, volume, lump, gob

예 *a huge ice mass*

inflate [infleit]　　　　　　　　　　부풀게 하다

뜻 exaggerate or make bigger

동 blow up, expand, amplify, swell, puff

예 *The charges were inflated*

---

insignificant [insignifikənt]　　　대수롭지 않은

뜻 not worthy of notice

동 undistinguished, trifling, trivial, negligible, unimportant

예 *insignificant sounds*

---

errand [erənd]　　　　　　　　　　심부름

뜻 a short trip that is taken in the performance of a necessary task or mission

동 mission, task, assignment, charge, job

예 *errand boy*

---

smooth [smuːð]　　　　　　　　　매끄러운

뜻 having a surface free from roughness or bumps or ridges or irregularities

동 unwrinkled, flowing, even, slick, soft

예 *smooth skin*

---

certificate [sərtifikət]　　　　　증명서

뜻 a document attesting to the truth of certain stated facts

동 certification, credential, credentials, testimonial, diploma

예 *he held several valuable securities*

---

relaxed [rilǽkst]　　　　　　　　긴장을 푼

뜻 without strain or anxiety

동 easygoing, carefree, loose, lax, tranquil

예 *gave the impression of being quite relaxed*

---

vast [væst, vɑ́:st]　　　　　　　　　　　　　　　　　　광대한

뜻 unusually great in size or amount or degree or especially extent or scope

동 huge, immense, Brobdingnagian, prodigious, broad

예 *the vast reaches of outer space*

---

totally [toutəli]　　　　　　　　　　　　　　　　　　　전적으로

뜻 to a complete degree or to the full or entire extent

동 wholly, entirely, completely, altogether, whole

예 *a totally new situation*

---

rush [rʌʃ]　　　　　　　　　　　　　　　　　　　　　돌진하다

뜻 move fast

동 hurry, dash, hasten, speed, run

예 *He rushed down the hall to receive his guests*

---

annoyance [ənɔ́iəns]　　　　　　　　　　　　　　　　　성가심

뜻 the psychological state of being irritated or annoyed

동 irritation, vexation, botheration, indignation, exasperation

예 *He expressed annoyance*

---

economic [ekənámik]　　　　　　　　　　　　　　　　　경제의

뜻 of or relating to an economy, the system of production and management of material wealth

동 economical, financial, commercial, fiscal, profitable

예 *economic growth*

---

wonder [wʌndər]　　　　　　　　　　　　이상하게 여기다, 놀라다

뜻 be amazed at

동 marvel, surprise, admire, be astonished, be startled

예 *We wondered at the child's linguistic abilities*

method [meθəd] 방법

㉟ a way of doing something, especially a systematic way

㊌ way, manner, mode, process, modus

㊌ *a new method*

---

specialize [speʃəlaiz] 전문화하다, 특수화하다

㉟ become more focus on an area of activity or field of study

㊌ specify, differentiate, particularize

㊌ *She specializes in Near Eastern history*

---

instinct [instiŋkt] 본능

㉟ inborn pattern of behavior often responsive to specific stimuli

㊌ aptitude, tendency, inclination, intuition

㊌ *the spawning instinct in salmon*

---

sense [sens] 감각

㉟ a general conscious awareness

㊌ feeling, sensibility, sensation, sensitivity

㊌ *a sense of security*

---

observation [àbzərveiʃən] 관찰

㉟ the act of observing

㊌ attention, remark, notice, investigation, surveillance

㊌ *observation deck*

---

vegetation [vedʒəteiʃən] 초목

㉟ all the plant life in a particular region or period

㊌ flora, botany, grasses, greenery, plants

㊌ *Pleistocene vegetation*

---

inferior [infɪəriər]   하위의

圏 of or characteristic of low rank or importance

圄 lower, subordinate, low, under, subsidiary

예 *inferior court*

---

achievement [ətʃiːvmənt]   달성

圏 the action of accomplishing something

圄 accomplishment, attainment, performance, success, fulfilment

예 *achievement test*

---

save [seiv]   모으다, 저축하다, 절약하다

圏 accumulate money for future use

圄 economize, amass, deposit, collect, gather

예 *He saves half his salary*

---

spank [spæŋk]   찰싹 때리다

圏 give a spanking to

圄 slap, beat, blip, clout, whip

예 *spank a child*

---

substance [sʌbstəns]   물질

圏 the real physical matter of which a person or thing consists

圄 entity, element, material, essence, stuff

예 *DNA is the substance of our genes*

---

steep [stiːp]   가파른

圏 having a sharp inclination

圄 sharp, perpendicular, precipitous, arduous, declivitous

예 *steep cliffs*

fixed [fikst]   고정된

图 fixed and unmoving

图 set, rigid, stationary, immovable, firm

예 *with eyes set in a fixed glassy stare*

---

cancellation [kænsəleiʃən]   말소, 해제

图 the act of cancelling

图 erasure, annulment, rescission, abolition, deletion

예 *cancellation law*

---

*Vocabulary/Expressions

Day 19

drought [draut]   가뭄

图 a shortage of rainfall

图 aridity, dryness, dry, aridness, parchedness

예 *Farmers most affected by the drought hope that there may yet be sufficient rain early in the growing season.*

---

reason [ri:zn]   이유

图 a rational motive for a belief or action

图 ground, cause, motive, occasion, excuse

예 *the reason that war was declared*

---

bless [bles]   축복하다

图 give a benediction to

图 sanctify, hallow, consecrate

예 *The dying man blessed his son.*

---

institute [instətju:t]   세우다, 설립하다

图 set up or lay the groundwork for

图 establish, found, plant, constitute, set up

예 *institute a new department*

---

sensitivity [sensətivəti]   민감도

图 responsiveness to external stimuli

图 sensitiveness, sensibility, impressionability, receptiveness

예 *sensitivity to pain*

---

assignment [əsainmənt]   할당

图 the act of distributing something to designated places or persons

图 assignation, allocation, allotment, quota, rationing

예 *The first task is the assignment of an address to each datum.*

---

confident [kánfədənt]   확신하고 있는

图 having or marked by confidence or assurance

图 sure, certain, assured, convinced, trusting

예 *a confident speaker*

---

incentive [insentiv]   유인, 동기

图 a positive motivational influence

图 inducement, motivator, stimulus, incitement, motivation

예 *incentive pay*

---

immature [imətʃuər]   미숙한

图 characteristic of a lack of maturity

图 unripe, young, inexperienced, puerile, jejune

예 *immature behavior*

---

obligate [ábləgeit]   강요하다

图 force somebody to do something

图 compel, oblige, constrain, coerce, bind

예 *We obligate all students to fill out this form.*

---

equality [ikwáləti]   같음, 동등

图 a state of being essentially equal or equivalent

图 equivalence, equation, par, similarity, identity

예 *on a equality with the best*

---

closeness [klousnis]   친밀, 근사

图 a feeling of being intimate and belonging together

图 intimacy, nearness, adjacency, propinquity, vicinity

예 *Their closeness grew as the night wore on.*

---

possession [pəzeʃən]   소유

图 the act of having and controlling property

图 ownership, tenure, holding, occupancy, occupation

예 *adverse possession*

---

stretch [stretʃ]   잡아 늘이다

图 extend one's limbs or muscles, or the entire body

图 extend, elongate, strain, spread, reach

예 *Stretch your legs*

---

marine [məriːn]   바다의

图 of or relating to the sea

图 maritime, aquatic, coastal, oceanic, Neptunian

예 *marine explorations*

---

consume [kənsuːm]   소비하다

图 use up (resources or materials)

图 expend, deplete, exhaust, spend, dissipate

예 *This car consumes a lot of gas.*

---

shame [ʃeim]   수치

图 a state of dishonor

图 disgrace, ignominy, opprobrium, obloquy, derision

예 *One mistake brought shame to all his family.*

---

growth [grouθ]   성장

图 the process of an individual organism growing organically

图 growing, maturation, development, increment, accretion

예 *He proposed an indicator of osseous growth in children.*

unambiguous [ʌnæmbigjuəs]   명백한
- 图 admitting of no doubt or misunderstanding
- 图 unequivocal, univocal, definite, apparent, obvious
- 예 *unambiguous evidence*

conversation [kànvərseiʃən]   회화, 대화
- 图 the use of speech for informal exchange of views or ideas or information etc.
- 图 dialogue, discourse, communication, speech, talk
- 예 *I have the conversation with him.*

deliberately [dilibərətli]   신중히, 고의로
- 图 with intention
- 图 intentionally, designedly, purposely, advisedly, measuredly
- 예 *He used that word deliberately.*

borrow [bárou]   빌리다
- 图 get temporarily
- 图 loan, lend, adopt, rent
- 예 *May I borrow your lawn mower.*

suit [suːt]   적합하다
- 图 be agreeable or acceptable to
- 图 accommodate, fit, match, adjust, befit
- 예 *This suits my needs.*

reservation [rezərveiʃən]   예약
- 图 the act of reserving (a place or passage) or engaging the services of (a person or group)
- 图 booking, appointment, preengagement, precontract
- 예 *I wondered who had made the reservation.*

exhibition [eksəbiʃən] 전시

- 의 the act of exhibiting
- 동 exposition, showing, display, exposure, demonstration
- 예 *a remarkable exhibition of musicianship*

adult [ədʌlt] 어른의

- 의 fully developed
- 동 developed, grown, grownup, mature
- 예 *an adult animal*

conclude [kənklu:d] 끝내다

- 의 come to a close
- 동 finish, end, terminate, complete, determine
- 예 *The concert closed with a nocturne by Chopin.*

anticipate [æntisəpeit] 예상하다

- 의 regard something as probable or likely
- 동 expect, foresee, forestall, await, predict
- 예 *The meteorologists are anticipating rain for tomorrow.*

edge [edʒ] 가장자리

- 의 a sharp side formed by the intersection of two surfaces of an object
- 동 brim, verge, brink, margin, rim
- 예 *He rounded the edges of the box.*

rustle [rʌsl] 살랑살랑 소리내다

- 의 make a dry crackling sound
- 동 sough, whisper, murmur, swish, crepitate
- 예 *rustling silk*

immigrant [imigrənt]   이주자

뜻 a person who comes to a country where they were not born in order to settle there

동 alien, settler, incomer, migrant

예 *quota immigrant*

---

career [kəriər]   경력

뜻 the general progression of your working or professional life

동 course, record, personal history, antecedent

예 *The general had had a distinguished career.*

---

occupy [ákjupai]   차지하다

뜻 occupy the whole of

동 fill, take, hold, possess

예 *The liquid fills the container.*

---

volume [válju:m]   부피

뜻 the amount of 3-dimensional space occupied by an object

동 bulk, capacity, size, mass

예 *The gas expanded to twice its original volume.*

---

region [ri:dʒən]   지역

뜻 a part of an animal that has a special function or is supplied by a given artery or nerve

동 area, district, territory, zone, land

예 *in the abdominal region*

---

found [faund]   설립하다

뜻 set up or found

동 establish, launch, institute, build, base

예 *She found a literacy program*

---

count [kaunt]　　　　　　　　　　　　세다

뜻 determine the number or amount of

동 number, enumerate, numerate, reckon, calculate

예 *Can you count the books on your shelf?*

meet [miːt]　　　　　　　　　　　　만나다

뜻 come together

동 see, encounter, come across,　run into

예 *I'll probably meet you at the meeting.*

single [siŋgl]　　　　　　　　　단 하나의

뜻 existing alone or consisting of one entity or part or aspect or individual

동 sole, only, solitary, singular, one

예 *a single survivor*

scale [skeil]　　　　　　　　　　　　규모

뜻 an ordered reference standard

동 measure, hierarchy, size, scope

예 *judging on a scale of 1 to 10*

endure [indjuər]　　　　　　　　　견디다

뜻 put up with something or somebody unpleasant

동 bear, stand, suffer, sustain, undergo

예 *The new secretary had to endure a lot of unprofessional remarks.*

explore [iksplɔːr]　　　　　　　　탐험하다

뜻 travel to or penetrate into

동 investigate, probe, examine, investigate, survey

예 *explore unknown territory in biology*

harsh [háːrʃ] 거친

- 图 unpleasantly stern
- 图 rough, coarse, gruff, crude, uneven
- 예 *wild and harsh country full of hot sand and cactus*

---

dictate [dikteit] 구술하다

- 图 say out loud for the purpose of recording
- 图 state, say, pronounce, instruct
- 예 *He dictated a report to his secretary.*

---

mark [máːrk] 표, 흔적

- 图 a distinguishing symbol
- 图 sign, token, stamp, brand
- 예 *The owner's mark was on all the sheep.*

---

victim [viktim] 희생자

- 图 a person who is tricked or swindled
- 图 sacrifice, casualty, sufferer, scapegoat, martyr
- 예 *He's the victim.*

---

habitation [hæbiteiʃən] 거주지

- 图 housing that someone is living in
- 图 dwelling, home, domicile, abode, residency
- 예 *He built a modest habitation near the pond.*

---

worthless [wɛːrθlis] 가치 없는

- 图 lacking in usefulness or value
- 图 valueless, useless, trashy, paltry, unworthy
- 예 *a worthless idler*

---

apply [əplai]   사용하다

囲 put into service

동 use, utilize, employ, utilise

예 *Apply a magnetic field here.*

---

optimism [áptəmizm]   낙천주의

囲 the optimistic feeling that all is going to turn out well

동 hopefulness, positivism, exhilaration, idealism

예 *I'm optimistic.*

---

situate [sitʃueit]   ...을 (어떤 장소·처지에) 놓다
- 뜻 determine or indicate the place, site, or limits of, as if by an instrument or by a survey
- 동 locate, place, position, put, set
- 예 *Situate the boundaries of the property.*

---

commercial [kəmɛːrʃəl]   상업상의
- 뜻 connected with or engaged in or sponsored by or used in commerce or commercial enterprises
- 동 economic, financial, fiscal, marketable, monetary
- 예 *commercial trucker*

---

salary [sǽləri]   봉급, 급료
- 뜻 something that remunerates
- 동 wage, pay, earnings, remuneration, income
- 예 *Salaries were paid by check.*

---

assure [əʃuər]   보증하다
- 뜻 make certain of
- 동 guarantee, ensure, insure, secure, convince
- 예 *This nest egg will assure a nice retirement for us.*

---

pioneer [paiəniər]   개척자, 선구자
- 뜻 someone who helps to open up a new line of research or technology or art
- 동 innovator, trailblazer, groundbreaker, trailblazer, pathfinder
- 예 *early pioneer*

---

provide [prəvaid]   공급하다
- 뜻 give something useful or necessary to
- 동 supply, render, furnish, replenish, serve
- 예 *We provided the room with an electrical heater.*

---

coherent [kouhiərənt]   조리가 서는

图 marked by an orderly, logical, and aesthetically consistent relation of parts

图 consistent, logical, ordered, understandable, comprehensible

예 *a coherent argument*

---

enemy [enəmi]   적

图 any hostile group of people

图 foe, foeman, opposition, opponent, rival

예 *He viewed lawyers as the real enemy.*

---

prefer [prifε :r]   오히려 ...을 좋아하다

图 like better

图 favor, select, choose, pick

예 *Some people prefer camping to staying in hotels.*

---

attract [ətrǽkt]   (주의·흥미 등을) 끌다

图 direct toward itself or oneself by means of some psychological power or physical attributes

图 pull, draw, allure, lure, tempt

예 *Her good looks attract the stares of many men.*

---

weaken [wi:kən]   약화시키다

图 lessen the strength of

图 abate, debilitate, invalidate, lessen, enervate

예 *The fever weakened his body.*

---

local [loukəl]   지방의

图 relating to or applicable to or concerned with the administration of a city or town or district rather than a larger area

图 topical, regional, native, sectional, provincial

예 *local taxes*

representative [reprizentətiv]   대표자

圈 a person who represents others

통 agent, delegate, deputy, proxy, exponent

예 *press representative*

---

awaken [əweikən]   깨우다

圈 cause to become awake or conscious

통 wake, waken, rouse, wake up, arouse

예 *He was awakened by the drunken men in the street.*

---

accountant [əkauntənt]   회계원

圈 someone who maintains and audits business accounts

통 bookkeeper, comptroller, controller, actuary, auditor

예 *public accountant*

---

honesty [ánisti]   정직

圈 the quality of being honest

통 integrity, rectitude, probity, sincerity, candor

예 *Honesty is the best policy.*

---

express [ikspres]   표현하다

圈 give expression to

통 show, evince, represent, utter, reveal

예 *She expressed her disappointment.*

---

deprive [dipraiv]   빼앗다

圈 take away possessions from someone

통 strip, divest, oust, seize, dispossess

예 *The Nazis deprived the Jews of all their assets.*

confidence [kánfədəns]   신임

图 freedom from doubt

图 assurance, belief, reliance, trust, faith

예 *After that failure he lost his confidence.*

---

need [ni:d]   필요

图 anything that is necessary but lacking

图 demand, want, requirement, necessity, desideratum

예 *She satisfied his need for affection*

---

deserve [dizɛ:rv]   ...할(받을) 만하다

图 be worthy or deserving

图 merit, earn, rate, be entitled to

예 *You deserve a promotion after all the hard work you have done.*

---

curious [kjuəriəs]   호기심이 강한

图 eager to investigate and learn or learn more

图 interested, inquisitive, questioning, inquiring

예 *A curious child is a teacher's delight.*

---

purchase [pɛ:rt ʃ əs]   사다

图 acquire by means of a financial transaction

图 buy, obtain, get, procure, take

예 *The family purchased a new car.*

---

earnest [ɛ:rnist]   진지한, 열심인

图 characterized by a firm and humorless belief in the validity of your opinions

图 sincere, solemn, ardent, eager, keen

예 *Both sides were deeply in earnest, even passionate.*

trivial [triviəl]　　　　　　　　하찮은
- 图 small and of little importan
- 图 fiddling, footling, piddling, piffling, insignificant
- 예 *a trivial matter*

rite [rait]　　　　　　　　의식
- 图 an established ceremony prescribed by a religion
- 图 ceremony, tradition, custom, ritual, service
- 예 *the rite of baptism*

aspiration [æspərei∫ən]　　　　　　　　포부
- 图 a cherished desire
- 图 ambition, dream, goal, aim, desire
- 예 *His aspiration is to own his own business.*

motive [moutiv]　　　　　　　　동기
- 图 the psychological feature that arouses an organism to action toward a desired goal
- 图 motivation, need, reason, incentive, inducement
- 예 *He acted with the best of motives.*

emission [imi∫ən]　　　　　　　　방사
- 图 the act of emitting
- 图 emanation, diffusion, issuance, ejection, radiation
- 예 *Emission of carbon dioxide*

alike [əlaik]　　　　　　　　비슷한
- 图 having the same or similar characteristics
- 图 like, analogous, corresponding, approximate, resembling
- 예 *All politicians are alike.*

compare [kəmpὲər]   비교하다

图 examine and note the similarities or differences of

图 collate

예 *We compared notes after we had both seen the movie.*

---

emerge [imὲ :rdʒ]   나타나다

图 come out into view, as from concealment

图 appear, arise, turn up, emanate, show

예 *Suddenly, the proprietor emerged from his office.*

---

treat [tri:t]   대우하다, 다루다

图 interact in a certain way

图 handle, deal with, manage, wield, cover

예 *Treat him with caution, please.*

---

bravery [breivəri]   용감

图 a quality of spirit that enables you to face danger or pain without showing fear

图 courage, courageousness, braveness, valor, nerve

예 *He was praised for bravery.*

---

odd [ád]   이상한

图 beyond or deviating from the usual or expected

图 peculiar, queer, funny, singular, weird

예 *I had an odd name.*

---

late [leit]   늦은

图 being or occurring at an advanced period of time or after a usual or expected time

图 belated, delayed, dilatory, tardy, overdue

예 *late evening*

cease [siːs]   그만두다

图 put an end to a state or an activity

图 discontinue, stop, give up, quit, halt

예 *Cease teasing your little brother*

---

competitive [kəmpetətiv]   경쟁의

图 involving competition or competitiveness

图 competitory, rival, emulous, competing, vying

예 *competitive games*

---

widespread [waidspred]   널리 보급된

图 widely circulated or diffused

图 extensive, comprehensive, broad, universal, prevalent

예 *a widespread doctrine*

---

trail [treil]   끌고 간 자국

图 a track or mark left by something that has passed

图 path, mark, trace, footprints, rut

예 *There is a trail of blood.*

---

reluctant [rilʌktənt]   마음 내키지 않는

图 unwillingness to do something contrary to your custom

图 loath, loth, unenthusiastic, unwilling, tardy

예 *a reluctant smile*

---

glare [glɛ̀ər]   섬광

图 a light within the field of vision that is brighter than the brightness to which the eyes are adapted

图 blaze, brilliance, dazzle, flame, glow

예 *a glare of sunlight*

---

arrangement [əreindʒmənt]　　　　　　　　정돈, 배열

图 an orderly grouping (of things or persons) considered as a unit

동 alignment, array, disposition, display, lineup

예 *a flower arrangement*

gloom [glu:m]　　　　　　　　　　　　　　어둠침침함

图 a state of partial or total darkness

동 somberness, blackness, obscurity, shadow, dimness

예 *He struck a match to dispel the gloom.*

apparatus [ə pərǽtəs]　　　　　　　　　　기구, 장치

图 equipment designed to serve a specific function

동 setup, device, implement, mechanism, tackle

예 *a wireless apparatus*

renew [rinju:]　　　　　　　　　　　　　　새롭게 하다

图 reestablish on a new, usually improved, basis or make new or like new

동 regenerate, refurbish, renovate, freshen, recreate

예 *They renewed their membership.*

upgrade [ʌpgreid]　　　　　　　　　　　품질을 개량하다

图 to improve what was old or outdated

동 advance, better, enhance, progress, ameliorate

예 *I've upgraded my computer so I can run better software.*

depress [dipres]　　　　　　　　　　　　낙담시키다

图 lower someone's spirits

동 deject, dismay, dispirit, discourage, oppress

예 *These news depressed her.*

strain [strein]   잡아당기다

뜻 use to the utmost

동 extend, stretch, distend, pull, tighten

예 *Don't strain your mind too much.*

---

population [pàpjuleiʃən]   인구, 주민수

뜻 the entire aggregation of items from which samples can be drawn

동 universe, people, populace, folk

예 *it is an estimate of the mean of the population.*

---

*Vocabulary/Expressions

Day 21

wretched [retʃid]   비참한

图 characterized by physical misery

동 miserable, woeful, abject, pitiful, calamitous

예 *I spent a wretched night on the floor.*

obtain [əbtein]   획득하다

图 come into possession of

동 get, acquire, attain, procure, take

예 *How did you obtain the visa?*

dramatically [drəmǽtikəli]   극적으로

图 in a very impressive manner

동 excessively, greatly, effectively, completely, definitely

예 *Your performance will improve dramatically.*

insight [insait]   통찰력

图 clear or deep perception of a situation

동 penetration, perceptivity, intuition, understanding, perspicacity

예 *She had an insight.*

reference [refərəns]   참조

图 a short note recognizing a source of information or of a quoted passage

동 citation, cite, mention, quotation

예 *The article includes reference of similar clinical cases.*

abstract [ǽbstrǽkt]   추상적인

图 existing only in the mind

동 conceptual, theoretical, notional, discrete, transcendental

예 *abstract words like `truth' and `justice'*

slight [slait]　　　　　　　　　　　　　　　　　　　근소한, 적은

图 small in quantity or degree

图 little, insignificant, minor, scanty, trifling

예 *There's slight chance that it will work.*

---

attention [ətenʃən]　　　　　　　　　　　　　　　　주의, 주목

图 the process whereby a person concentrates on some features of the environment to the (relative) exclusion of others

图 concentration, intentness, contemplation, immersion, notice

예 *give attention to*

---

wipe [waip]　　　　　　　　　　　　　　　　　　　　닦다

图 rub with a circular motion

图 dry, mop, swab, clean, erase

예 *wipe the blackboard*

---

sake [seik]　　　　　　　　　　　　　　　　　위함, 목적, 이유

图 a reason for wanting something done

图 interest, reason, objective, aim, cause

예 *He died for the sake of his country.*

---

frown [fraun]　　　　　　　　　　　　　　　　눈살을 찌푸리다

图 look angry or sullen, wrinkle one's forehead, as if to signal disapproval

图 scowl, grimace, glower, sulk, pout

예 *She frowned at him.*

---

drag [dræg]　　　　　　　　　　　　　　　　　　　　끌다

图 pull, as against a resistance

图 attract, draw, draft, haul, trail

예 *He dragged the big suitcase behind him.*

dialogue [daiələ(:)g] 대화
国 a conversation between two persons
동 conversation, discourse, communication, speech, talk
예 *I have the dialogue with him.*

assimilation [əsiməlei ʃ ən] 동화
国 the state of being assimilated
동 anabolism, assimilate, adaptation, anabolism
예 *progressive assimilation*

incorrect [inkərekt] 부정확한
国 not correct
동 wrong, inaccurate, imprecise, inexact, unsuitable
예 *an incorrect calculation*

nervous [nɛ :rvəs] 두려워하는, 불안한
国 causing or fraught with or showing anxiety
동 anxious, queasy, uneasy, unquiet, fearful
예 *those nervous moments before takeoff*

variable [vɛ̀əriəbl] 변하기 쉬운
国 liable to or capable of change
동 changeable, mutable, fickle, inconstant, unsteady
예 *variable expenses*

craft [kræft] 기능
国 the skilled practice of a practical occupation
동 skill, technique, ingenuity, art, proficiency
예 *He learned his trade as an apprentice.*

wander [wɑ́ndər]   돌아다니다

뜻 move about aimlessly or without any destination, often in search of food or employment

동 roam, rove, ramble, stray, stroll

예 *the wandering Jew*

---

sensibility [sensəbiləti]   민감

뜻 responsiveness to external stimuli

동 sensitivity, susceptibility, sensitiveness, delicacy, sensitiveness

예 *sensitivity to pain*

---

extremely [ikstriːmli]   극단적으로

뜻 to a high degree or extent

동 highly, exceedingly, very, immensely, greatly

예 *extremely interesting*

---

demand [dimǽnd]   요구하다

뜻 request urgently and forcefully

동 ask, require, claim, request, call for

예 *The victim's family is demanding compensation.*

---

expense [ikspéns]   지출, 비용

뜻 amounts paid for goods and services that may be currently tax deductible

동 disbursal, expenditure, cost, outlay, charge

예 *administrative expense*

---

envious [énviəs]   시기심이 강한

뜻 showing extreme cupidity

동 covetous, jealous, desirous, green-eyed, jaundiced

예 *envious of their art collection*

---

embarrassed [imbǽrəst]　　　　　　　　난처한
医 feeling or caused to feel uneasy and self-conscious

동 abashed, chagrined, confused, shamefaced, ashamed

예 *She was embarrassed by her child's tantrums.*

---

accessible [æksésəbl]　　　　　　　접근하기 쉬운
医 capable of being reached

동 approachable, operative, open, getatable, exposed

예 *a town accessible by rail*

---

drift [drı́ft]　　　　　　　　　　　표류하다
医 be in motion due to some air or water current

동 float, be adrift, blow, sail

예 *The boat drifted on the lake.*

---

biography [baiágrəfi]　　　　　　　　　전기
医 an account of the series of events making up a person's life

동 life story, life history, life, memoir, personal anecdote

예 *campaign biography*

---

leak [lı́:k]　　　　　　　　　　　　　새다
医 enter or escape as through a hole or crack or fissure

동 ooze, seep, trickle, spill, get out

예 *Water leaked out of the can into the backpack.*

---

contact [kántækt]　　　　　　　　　　접촉
医 the act of touching physically

동 touch, connection, junction, tangency, contingence

예 *Her fingers came in contact with the light switch*

physical [fízikəl]   육체의, 신체의

뜻 involving the body as distinguished from the mind or spirit

동 bodily, corporeal, corporal, fleshly

예 *physical exercise*

---

collection [kəlékʃən]   수집

뜻 the act of gathering something together

동 collecting, assembling, aggregation, accumulation, gathering

예 *data collection*

---

factory [fæktəri]   공장

뜻 a plant consisting of one or more buildings with facilities for manufacturing

동 plant, mill, works, manufactory, foundry

예 *factory automation*

---

literate [lítərət]   글을 읽고 쓸 줄 아는

뜻 able to read and write

동 educated, lettered, learned, cultivated, cultured

예 *literate person*

---

means [mí:nz]   방법, 수단

뜻 how a result is obtained or an end is achieved

동 way, medium, method, mode, step

예 *a means of control*

---

dominate [dámənèit]   지배하다

뜻 have dominance or the power to defeat over

동 master, predominate, rule, reign, control

예 *Her pain completely dominated her.*

---

multiple [mʌltəpl] 복합적인
图 having or involving or consisting of more than one part or entity or individual
图 manifold, multifarious, diversified, varied, various
예 *multiple ownership*

chant [tʃænt] (노래, 성가를) 부르다
图 recite with musical intonation
图 intone, intonate, cantillate, sing, recite
예 *The rabbi chanted a prayer.*

selfless [sélflis] 사심없는, 무욕의
图 showing unselfish concern for the welfare of others
图 altruistic, unselfish, disinterested, magnanimous, generous
예 *selfless present*

guilty [gílti] 유죄의
图 responsible for or chargeable with a reprehensible act
图 culpable, delinquent, sinful, blameworthy, peccant
예 *guilty of murder*

client [klàiənt] 고객
图 someone who pays for goods or services
图 customer, patron, regular, buyer, user
예 *He is my client.*

kingdom [kíŋdəm] 왕국, 왕토
图 a domain in which something is dominant
图 realm, empire, monarchy
예 *the untroubled kingdom of reason*

penalty [pénəlti]　　　　　　　　　　　　　　형벌

圐 the act of punishing

圄 punishment, penalization, penalisation, castigation, retribution

剛 *death penalty*

---

decrease [dikríːs]　　　　　　　　　　　　감소하다

圐 decrease in size, extent, or range

圄 diminish, lessen, fall, reduce, decline

剛 *The amount of homework decreased towards the end of the semester*

---

accommodation [əkàmədéiʃən]　　　　　숙박 설비

圐 living quarters provided for public convenience

圄 housing, lodging, staying, billeting

剛 *overnight accommodations are available*

---

efficient [ifíʃənt]　　　　　　　　　　　능률적인

圐 being effective without wasting time or effort or expense

圄 effective, efficacious, capable, effectual, productive

剛 *an efficient production manager*

---

apparent [əpǽrənt]　　　　　　　　　　명백한

圐 clearly revealed to the mind or the senses or judgment

圄 evident, manifest, plain, unmistakable, clear

剛 *The effects of the drought are apparent to anyone who sees the parched fields.*

---

resolution [rèzəlúːʃən]　　　　　　　　　결정

圐 something settled or resolved

圄 settlement, closure, determination, decision, verdict

剛 *They never did achieve a final resolution of their differences.*

---

obtainable [əbtéinəbl]   얻을 수 있는

医 capable of being obtained

图 gettable, getable, procurable, available, attainable

예 *Savings of up to 50 percent are obtainable.*

---

temperament [témpərəmənt]   기질

医 your usual mood

图 disposition, mettle, nature, character, personality

예 *He has a happy temperament.*

---

*Vocabulary/Expressions

Day 22

---

nourishing [nɑːriʃiŋ]   자양이 되는

뜻 of or providing nourishment

동 alimentary, alimental, nutrient, nutritious, nutritive

예 *good nourishing stew*

---

inaccurate [inǽkjurət]   부정확한

뜻 not exact

동 erroneous, fallacious, false, faulty, wrong

예 *an inaccurate translation*

---

regulate [regjuleit]   규제하다

뜻 bring into conformity with rules or principles or usage

동 control, regularize, govern, manage, rule

예 *We cannot regulate the way people dress.*

---

exclaim [ikskleim]   외치다

뜻 utter aloud

동 cry, outcry, shout, holler, whoop

예 *I won! he exclaimed.*

---

sympathize [simpəθaiz]   동정하다

뜻 to feel or express sympathy or compassion

동 commiserate, pity, compassionate, console, condole

예 *You must sympathize the widow.*

---

term [təːrm]   용어

뜻 a word or expression used for some particular thing

동 language, terminology, nomenclature, wording

예 *He learned many medical terms.*

---

preparation [prepərei ʃ ən]   준비

- 뜻 the cognitive process of thinking about what you will do in the event of something happening
- 동 readiness, planning, preparedness, arrangements, provision
- 예 *His preparation for retirement was hindered by several uncertainties.*

maddening [mǽdniŋ]   미치게 하는

- 뜻 extremely annoying or displeasing
- 동 exasperating, infuriating, vexing, irritating, annoying
- 예 *The ceaseless tumult of the jukebox was maddening.*

hitch [hit ʃ]   걸다

- 뜻 to hook or entangle
- 동 catch, fasten, attach, tie, join
- 예 *One foot hitched in the stirrup.*

eternally [itə :rnəli]   영원히

- 뜻 for a limitless time
- 동 everlastingly, forever, evermore, endlessly, perpetually
- 예 *No one can live eternally.*

tax [tǽks]   세금

- 뜻 charge against a citizen's person or property or activity for the support of government
- 동 taxation, duty, impost, imposition, custom
- 예 *additional tax*

assist [əsist]   돕다

- 뜻 give help or assistance
- 동 aid, succor, support, befriend, relieve
- 예 *Everyone assisted out during the earthquake.*

hesitate [hezəteit]   주저하다

- 图 pause or hold back in uncertainty or unwillingness
- 동 falter, halt, pause, scruple, waver
- 예 *Authorities hesitate to quote exact figures.*

---

chew [t ʃ uː]   씹다

- 图 to bite and grind with the teeth
- 동 munch, masticate, manducate, jaw, champ
- 예 *Chew your food and don't swallow it!*

---

permanent [pɑ ːrmənənt]   영구적인

- 图 continuing or enduring without marked change in status or condition or place
- 동 lasting, constant, steady, standing, everlasting
- 예 *permanent secretary to the president*

---

accomplish [əkámpli ʃ]   이루다, 성취하다

- 图 to gain with effort
- 동 achieve, attain, reach, fulfil, perform
- 예 *She accomplished her goal despite setbacks.*

---

quit [kwit]   그만두다

- 图 put an end to a state or an activity
- 동 discontinue, stop, cease, give up, leave
- 예 *Quit teasing your little brother.*

---

necessity [nəsesəti]   필수품

- 图 anything indispensable
- 동 essential, requirement, requisite, necessary, need
- 예 *Food and shelter are necessities of life.*

daily [deili]　　　　　　　　　　　　　　　　　　　매일의
- 뜻 of or belonging to or occurring every day
- 동 everyday, quotidian, diurnal, day-to-day
- 예 daily routine

ceremony [serəmouni]　　　　　　　　　　　　　　의식
- 뜻 a formal event performed on a special occasion
- 동 ritual, observance, solemnity, rite, service
- 예 a ceremony commemorating Pearl Harbor

scary [skὲəri]　　　　　　　　　　　　　　　　　무서운
- 뜻 provoking fear terror
- 동 chilling, scarey, terrible, dreadful, fearful
- 예 a scary movie

register [redʒistər]　　　　　　　　　등록하다, 기록하다
- 뜻 enroll to vote
- 동 record, enter, enrol, list, entry
- 예 register for an election

satisfactory [sætisfǽktəri]　　　　　　　　만족스러운
- 뜻 giving satisfaction
- 동 satisfying, adequate, sufficient, gratifying, pleasing
- 예 satisfactory living conditions

barter [bάːrtər]　　　　　　　　　　　　　물물교환하다
- 뜻 exchange goods without involving money
- 동 exchange, swap, swop, trade, interchange
- 예 exchange and barter

relationship [rilei ʃ ən ʃ ip] 관계

圐 a relation between people

圄 connection, kinship, association, bond, contact

圀 *the relationship between mothers and their children*

---

contain [kəntein] 포함하다

圐 have as a component

圄 incorporate, comprise, include, involve, embody

圀 *The record contains many old songs from the 1930's.*

---

examination [igzæ mənei ʃ ən] 조사

圐 the act of examining something closely

圄 scrutiny, inspection, investigation, survey, research

圀 *direct examination*

---

dribble [dribl] 똑똑 떨어뜨리다

圐 run or flow slowly, as in drops or in an unsteady stream

圄 trickle, drip, drop, ooze

圀 *Reports began to dribble in.*

---

deed [diːd] 행위

圐 something that people do or cause to happen

圄 act, action, work, doing, feat

圀 *a bad deed*

---

scout [skaut] 정찰병

圐 a person employed to keep watch for some anticipated event

圄 lookout, sentinel, sentry, spotter, picket

圀 *scout car*

yell [jel] 큰소리를 지르다

医 utter a sudden loud cry

同 shout, cry, call, scream, holler

예 *I yelled to her from the window but she couldn't hear me*

---

intend [intend] 의도하다

医 mean or intend to express or convey

同 purpose, design, plan, aim, think

예 *What do his words intend?*

---

discard [diská:rd] 버리다

医 throw or cast away

同 fling, toss, dispose, abandon, dismiss

예 *Discard your worries.*

---

contrary [kántreri] 반대의

医 very opposed in nature or character or purpose

同 opposite, adverse, reverse, counter, opponent

예 *acts contrary to our code of ethics*

---

dietary [daiəteri] 식이 요법의

医 of or relating to the diet

同 dietetic, dietetical, alimentary

예 *dietary restrictions*

---

survive [sərvaiv] 살아남다

医 continue to live through hardship or adversity

同 outlive, overlive, last, endure, live on

예 *These superstitions survive in the backwaters of America.*

---

distinctive [distiŋktiv]   특유의, 특색 있는

图 of a feature that helps to distinguish a person or thing

동 characteristic, peculiar, specific, special, typical

예 *Jerusalem has a distinctive Middle East flavor- Curtis Wilkie.*

---

folk [fouk]   사람들

图 people in general

동 nation, public, population, kindred, nationality

예 *They're just country folk.*

---

ease [iːz]   편함, 안정

图 freedom from difficulty or hardship or effort

동 easiness, comfort, relief, convenience, facility

예 *He rose through the ranks with apparent ease.*

---

interchange [intərt ʃ eindʒ]   서로 교환하다

图 put in the place of another

동 substitute, replace, exchange, swop, swap

예 *Synonyms can be interchanged without a changing the context's meaning.*

---

function [fʌŋk ʃ ən]   기능

图 what something is used for

동 purpose, role, use, ability, capacity

예 *The function of an auger is to bore holes.*

---

dawn [dɔːn]   새벽, 여명

图 the first light of day

동 dawning, morning, aurora, daybreak, dayspring

예 *We got up before dawn.*

secure [sikjuər]   안전한

圀 free from danger or risk

图 safe, sure, steady, guarded, riskless

예 *secure from harm*

---

report [ripɔːrt]   보고서

圀 a written document describing the findings of some individual or group

图 study, account, statement, paper, note

예 *This accords with the recent report by Hill and Dale.*

---

ethic [eθik]   도덕

圀 the principles of right and wrong that are accepted by an individual or a social group

图 morality, conscience, moral, morals, virtue

예 *the Puritan ethic*

---

alive [əlaiv]   살아 있는

圀 possessing life

图 living, brisk, animated, active, vivid

예 *The nerve is alive.*

---

sell [sel]   팔다

圀 exchange or deliver for money or its equivalent

图 vend, market, turn away, retail, dump

예 *These books sell like hot cakes.*

---

swing [swiŋ]   흔들리다

圀 move or walk in a swinging or swaying manner

图 sway, pendulate, dangle, oscillate, shake

예 *He swung back.*

---

react [riǽkt]   반작용하다, 반동하다

뜻 act against or in opposition to

동 oppose, counter, recoil, rebound, boomerang

예 *She reacts negatively to everything I say.*

---

distribute [distribjuːt]   분배하다

뜻 give to several people

동 divide, dispense, apportion, allot, hand out

예 *The teacher distributed out the exams.*

---

*Vocabulary/Expressions   Day 23

temperate [témpərət]   절제하는
- 뜻 not extreme in behavior
- 동 moderate, abstemious, restrained, abstinent, mild
- 예 *temperate in his habits*

---

besides [bisáidz]   게다가
- 뜻 making an additional point
- 동 moreover, furthermore, also, further, in addition
- 예 *I don't want to go to a restaurant besides, we can't afford it.*

---

shift [ʃift]   물건을 이동시키다
- 뜻 move around
- 동 transfer, take, transmit, remove
- 예 *Transfer the packet from his trouser pockets to a pocket in his jacket.*

---

contract [kántrækt]   계약
- 뜻 a binding agreement between two or more persons that is enforceable by law
- 동 covenant, treaty, pact, convention, engagement
- 예 *breach of contract*

---

fundamentally [fʌndəméntəli]   근본적으로
- 뜻 in essence
- 동 basically, essentially, radically, undoubtedly, certainly
- 예 *He is fundamentally dishonest.*

---

destiny [déstəni]   운명
- 뜻 an event (or a course of events) that will inevitably happen in the future
- 동 fate, lot, fortune, doom, kismet
- 예 *We are helpless in the face of destiny.*

---

mere [miər]   단순한

图 without additions or modifications

图 simple, plain, easy, uncomplicated, facile

例 *shocked by the mere idea*

---

resource [riːsɔːrs]   자원

图 a source of aid or support that may be drawn upon when needed

图 assets, property, reserve, reservoir, store

例 *The local library is a valuable resource.*

---

scratch [skrǽtʃ]   할퀴다

图 cause friction

图 scrape, scrabble, damage, lacerate, incise

例 *my sweater scratches*

---

obvious [ábviəs]   명백한

图 easily perceived by the senses or grasped by the mind

图 apparent, evident, manifest, plain, clear

例 *obvious errors*

---

numeral [njuːmərəl]   숫자

图 a symbol used to represent a number

图 figure, digit, cipher, digit

例 *He learned to write the numerals before he went to school.*

---

outlook [autluk]   견해

图 a habitual or characteristic mental attitude that determines how you will interpret and respond to situations

图 viewpoint, perspective, attitude, standpoint, angle

例 *There are pretty different in outlook.*

Day 23

plain [plein]   명백한

- 医 clearly revealed to the mind or the senses or judgment
- 동 apparent, evident, manifest, patent, obvious
- 예 *It is plain that he is no reactionary.*

patriotism [peitriətizm]   애국심

- 医 love of country and willingness to sacrifice for it
- 동 nationalism, chauvinism, allegiance, loyalty, public spirit
- 예 *They rode the same wave of popular patriotism.*

shield [ʃiːld]   보호하다

- 医 protect, hide, or conceal from danger or harm
- 동 defend, guard, cover, shelter, safeguard
- 예 *I couldn't shield her.*

remodel [riːmádl]   개조하다

- 医 cast or model anew
- 동 recast, reforge, reconstruct, redo, alter
- 예 *She had to remodel her image to please the electorate in her home state.*

honor [ánər]   명예

- 医 the state of being honored
- 동 esteem, fame, renown, glory, prestige
- 예 *She is an honor to the company.*

lay [lei]   놓다

- 医 put into a certain place or abstract location
- 동 set, place, pose, position, settle
- 예 *Lay your things here.*

suburb [sʌbəːrb] 교외

図 a residential district located on the outskirts of a city

동 outskirts, environs, suburbia, the burbs

예 *bedroom suburb*

---

struggle [strʌgl] 분투하다, 애쓰다

図 to exert strenuous effort against opposition

동 fight, strive, combat, endeavor, toil

예 *He struggled to get free from the rope.*

---

revise [rivaiz] 교정하다

図 make revisions in

동 review, amend, correct, alter, modify

예 *revise a thesis*

---

bargain [báːrgən] 매매 계약, 거래

図 an agreement between parties (usually arrived at after discussion) fixing obligations of each

동 deal, transaction, contract, stipulation, engagement

예 *He made a bargain with the devil.*

---

definite [defənit] 명확한

図 explicit and clearly defined

동 precise, certain, explicit, clear, determinate

예 *I want a definite answer.*

---

ignorant [ignərənt] 무지한

図 lacking knowledge or sophistication

동 uneducated, nescient, uninformed, unenlightened, mindless

예 *an ignorant man*

adolescent [ædəlesnt] 청소년기의

图 relating to or peculiar to or suggestive of an adolescent

동 youthful, young, juvenile, teenage, immature

예 *adolescent problems*

---

ultimately [ʌltəmətli] 최후로, 마침내

图 as the end result of a succession or process

동 finally, in the end, at last, eventually, lastly

예 *Ultimately he had to give in.*

---

lie [lai] 눕다

图 be lying, be prostrate

동 recline, loll, sprawl, stretch out

예 *The sick man lay in bed all day.*

---

twofold [tuːfould] 2배의, 이중의

图 having more than one decidedly dissimilar aspects or qualities

동 double, dual, bifold, binal, diploid

예 *The office of a clergyman is twofold; public preaching and private influence*

---

complete [kəmpliːt] 완료하다

图 come or bring to a finish or an end

동 finish, terminate, conclude, accomplish, consummate

예 *She completed the requirements for her Master's Degree*

---

misunderstand [misʌndərstǽnd] 오해하다

图 interpret in the wrong way

동 misconstrue, misinterpret, misconceive, misapprehend, miscomprehend

예 *She misunderstanded my remarks.*

---

protective [prətéktiv]　　　　　　　　　　　보호하는

图 intended or adapted to afford protection of some kind

동 defensive, preventive, guarding, securing, shielding

예 *a protective covering*

---

exotic [igzátik]　　　　　　　　　　　　　이국적인

图 being or from or characteristic of another place or part of the world

동 alien, outlandish, strange, foreign, peregrine

예 *exotic plants in a greenhouse*

---

monotonous [mənátənəs]　　　　　　　　단조로운

图 tediously repetitious or lacking in variety

동 humdrum, monotone, drab, tedious, unvaried

예 *Nothing is so monotonous as the sea.*

---

admirable [ædmərəbl]　　　　　　　　칭찬할 만한

图 deserving of the highest esteem or admiration

동 estimable, wonderful, marvellous, commendable, meritorious

예 *His taste was impeccable, his health admirable.*

---

dismiss [dismís]　　　　　　　　　　　해고하다

图 discharge from an office or position

동 displace, fire, terminate, lay off, turn off

예 *The boss dismissed his secretary today.*

---

hoop [hu:p]　　　　　　　　　　　　　　테

图 a rigid circular band of metal or wood or other material used for holding or fastening or hanging or pulling

동 ring, circle, rim, loop, circlet

예 *There was still a rusty iron hoop for tying a horse.*

---

mixture [mikstʃər]   혼합

圏 a substance consisting of two or more substances mixed together

동 blend, medley, compound, amalgam, melange

예 *He drank a mixture of beer and lemonade.*

---

choose [tʃuːz]   고르다

圏 pick out from a number of alternatives

동 take, select, pick, opt, cull

예 *Choose a good husband for your daughter*

---

mate [meit]   동료

圏 a fellow member of a team

동 partner, companion, teammate, friend, pal

예 *It was his first start against his former mates.*

---

visible [vizəbl]   명백한

圏 obvious to the eye

동 apparent, evident, obvious, noticeable, manifest

예 *a visible change of expression*

---

construction [kənstrʌkʃən]   건설

圏 the act of constructing something

동 building, structure, erection, establishment

예 *During the construction we had to take a detour.*

---

opposite [ápəzit]   반대편의

圏 being directly across from each other

동 contrary, reverse, converse, opposed, adverse

예 *at opposite poles*

---

skill [skil]   솜씨

- 图 an ability that has been acquired by training
- 图 accomplishment, acquirement, acquisition, attainment, knack
- 예 *the skill of a well-trained boxer*

---

glory [glɔːri]   영광, 명예

- 图 a state of high honor
- 图 splendor, fame, kudos, renown, dignity
- 예 *He valued glory above life itself.*

---

hardness [háːrdnis]   단단함

- 图 the property of being rigid and resistant to pressure
- 图 firmness, rigidity, toughness, stiffness, stability
- 예 *the hardness of stone*

---

slave [sleiv]   노예

- 图 a person who is owned by someone
- 图 thrall, helot, serf, bondservant, bondman
- 예 *slave to cocaine*

---

starting [stáːrtiŋ]   출발, 개시

- 图 a turn to be a starter
- 图 start, beginning, opening, outset, origin
- 예 *His starting meant that the coach thought he was one of their best linemen.*

---

luxury [lʌkʃəri]   사치

- 图 something that is an indulgence rather than a necessity
- 图 pomp, extravagance, lavishness, sumptuousness, luxuriousness
- 예 *luxury tax*

Day 23

patience [peiʃəns]   인내

- 图 good-natured tolerance of delay or incompetence
- 동 forbearance, longanimity, endurance, sufferance, solitaire
- 예 *Patience is a virtue.*

---

supreme [səpriːm]   최고의

- 图 highest in excellence or achievement
- 동 paramount, sovereign, top, utmost, superlative
- 예 *supreme among musicians*

---

*Vocabulary/Expressions

Day 24

daring [dɛ̀əriŋ]   용기, 대담성
- 뜻 a challenge to do something dangerous or foolhardy
- 동 boldness, audacity, courage, hardihood, hardiness
- 예 *He could never refuse a daring*

deluxe [dəluks]   호화로운
- 뜻 rich and superior in quality
- 동 grand, luxurious, opulent, princely, elegant
- 예 *deluxe dining rooms*

internal [intə:rnl]   내부의
- 뜻 happening or arising or located within some limits or especially surface
- 동 inner, interior, inward, inside, indoor
- 예 *internal organs*

represent [reprizent]   나타내다
- 뜻 express indirectly by an image, form, or model
- 동 typify, symbolize, depict, show, describe
- 예 *What does the Statue of Liberty represent?*

ridiculous [ridikjuləs]   웃기는
- 뜻 inviting ridicule
- 동 absurd, laughable, ludicrous, funny, comical
- 예 *Her conceited assumption of universal interest in her rather dull children was ridiculous.*

manage [mǽnidʒ]   관리하다
- 뜻 be in charge of, act on, or dispose of
- 동 handle, deal, administer, govern, direct
- 예 *She managed her parents' affairs after they got too old.*

Day 24

purpose [pɛ:rpəs]   목적
图 an anticipated outcome that is intended or that guides your planned actions
图 intent, intention, aim, design, object
예 *His purpose was to provide a new translation.*

reverse [rivɛ:rs]   반대
图 a relation of direct opposition
图 contrary, opposite, objection, dissension, dissent
예 *We thought Sue was older than Bill but just the reverse was true.*

genius [dʒi:njəs]   천재, 비범한 재능
图 someone who has exceptional intellectual ability and originality
图 prodigy, wizard, brain, mastermind, ability
예 *Mozart was a child genius.*

extent [ikstent]   범위, 정도
图 the point or degree to which something extends
图 scope, range, degree, measure, magnitude
예 *the extent of the damage*

mission [miʃən]   사명, 임무
图 a special assignment that is given to a person or group
图 charge, commission, errand, task, vocation
예 *a confidential mission to London*

shake [ʃeik]   흔들다
图 move or cause to move back and forth
图 agitate, tremble, shiver, quake, jolt
예 *The chemist shook the flask vigorously.*

repair [ripέər]   수리하다

图 restore by replacing a part or putting together what is torn or broken

동 mend, fix, refit, correct, redress

예 *She repaired her TV set.*

---

revision [riviʒən]   개정

图 the act of revising or altering

동 alteration, review, correction, revise, change

예 *It would require a drastic revision of his opinion.*

---

reservoir [rezərvwɑ̀:r]   (지식·부 등의) 저장

图 a large or extra supply of something

동 accumulation, storage, preservation, save, store

예 *a reservoir of talent*

---

require [rikwaiər]   필요로 하다

图 have need of

동 necessitate, want, need, desire, wish

예 *Success usually requires hard work.*

---

accompany [əkʌmpəni]   동반하다

图 be present or associated with an event or entity

동 attend, escort, go with, come with

예 *Heart attacks are accompanied by distruction of heart tissue.*

---

scenery [si:nəri]   풍경

图 the appearance of a place

동 decor, landscape, spectacle, view, vista

예 *picturesque scenery*

---

invariably [invɛ̀əriəbli]　　　　　　　　　변함없이

国 without variation or change, in every case

届 constantly, always, permanently, perpetually, eternally

예 *invariably kind and gracious*

---

erect [irekt]　　　　　　　　　　　　　똑바로 선

国 upright in position or posture

届 vertical, straight, upstanding, perpendicular, plumb

예 *an erect stature*

---

oral [ɔ:rəl]　　　　　　　　　　　　　　구두의

国 using speech rather than writing

届 verbal, vocal, nuncupative, spoken

예 *an oral agreement*

---

expectation [ekspektei ʃ ən]　　　　　기대, 예상

国 anticipating with confidence of fulfillment

届 expectancy, expectance, hope, anticipation, prospect

예 *Expectation Sunday*

---

claim [kleim]　　　　　　　　　　　　요구하다

国 demand as being one's due or property

届 require, call for, postulate, need, challenge

예 *He claimed his suitcases at the airline counter.*

---

role [roul]　　　　　　　　　　　　　　역할

国 the actions and activities assigned to or required or expected of a person or group

届 part, function, position

예 *play its role*

---

transport [trænspɔːrt]

수송하다

図 move while supporting, either in a vehicle or in one's hands or on one's body

图 carry, convey, haul, transfer, ship

예 *You must transport your camping gear.*

foster [fɔːstər]

육성하다

図 promote the growth of

图 bring up, nurture, raise, nourish, cherish

예 *foster our children's well-being and education*

sensitive [sensətiv]

민감한

図 responsive to physical stimuli

图 susceptible, touchy, delicate, tender, impressionable

예 *sensitive skin*

document [dákjumənt]

문서, 서류

図 writing that provides information

图 paper, writing, letters, record, archives, report

예 *my documents*

domestic [dəmestik]

국내의, 자국의

図 of concern to or concerning the internal affairs of a nation

图 national, native, indigenous, municipal, inland

예 *domestic issues such as tax rate and highway construction*

spirit [spirit]

정신, 마음

図 the state of a person's emotions

图 soul, mind, psyche, attitude, consciousness

예 *He was in good spirits.*

grade [greid] 등급

囹 a relative position or degree of value in a graded group

图 level, degree, rank, class, rating

예 *lumber of the highest grade*

---

similar [simələr] 비슷한

囹 marked by correspondence or resemblance

图 like, alike, analogous, comparable, equivalent

예 *similar food at similar prices*

---

annoy [ənɔi] 성가시게 굴다

囹 disturb, especially by minor irritations

图 bother, irritate, tease, pester, irk

예 *Mosquitoes buzzing in my ear really annoyed me.*

---

publish [pʌbliʃ] 발표하다

囹 prepare and issue for public distribution or sale

图 issue, release, promulgate, announce, proclaim

예 *publish a magazine or newspaper*

---

expression [ikspreʃən] 표현

囹 the communication (in speech or writing) of your beliefs or opinions

图 phrase, verbalism, express, presentation, statement

예 *expressions of good will*

---

determination [ditɑ:rməneiʃən] 결정, 결심

囹 a position or opinion or judgment reached after consideration

图 decision, conclusion, resolution, closure, settlement

예 *satisfied with the panel's determination*

instruction [instrʌkʃən]
뜻 activities that impart knowledge or skill
동 education, teaching, pedagogy, didactics, training
예 *Our instruction was carefully programmed.*

교육

resemble [rizembl]
뜻 appear like
동 take after, look like, be like, be similar to, be alike
예 *She resembles her mother very much.*

...을 닮다

suitable [suːtəbl]
뜻 meant or adapted for an occasion or use
동 suited, fit, appropriate, proper, apt
예 *a tractor suitable for heavy duty*

적당한

multiply [mʌltəplai]
뜻 combine or increase by multiplication
동 propagate, augment, enlarge, heighten, proliferate
예 *He managed to multiply his profits.*

증가시키다

reconcile [rekənsail]
뜻 make one thing compatible with another
동 accommodate, conciliate, adjust, attune, regulate
예 *The scientists had to reconcile the new results with the existing theories.*

조정하다, 중재하다

breast [brest]
뜻 rich and superior in quality
동 bosom, chest, bust, heart
예 *deluxe dining rooms*

가슴

prejudice [predʒudis]   편견, 선입관

- 医 a partiality that prevents objective consideration of an issue or situation
- 동 bias, preconception, prepossession, partiality, distorted views
- 예 *a bad prejudice*

---

solitary [sάləteri]   혼자의

- 医 being the only one
- 동 sole, single, singular, one, only
- 예 *a solitary instance of cowardice*

---

substitute [sΛbstətjuːt]   대신하다

- 医 put in the place of another
- 동 exchange, displace, interchange, replace, supersede
- 예 *substitute regular milk with fat-free milk*

---

threat [θret]   위협

- 医 something that is a source of danger
- 동 menace, intimidation, compulsion, duress, pressure
- 예 *Earthquakes are a constant threat in Japan.*

---

exaggerate [igzǽdʒəreit]   과장하다

- 医 do something to an excessive degree
- 동 overdo, hyperbolize, magnify, overstate, overdraw
- 예 *He exaggerated it last night when he did 100 pushups.*

---

obligation [àbləgeiʃən]   의무

- 医 the social force that binds you to the courses of action demanded by that force
- 동 duty, responsibility, commitment, liability, onus
- 예 *We must instill a sense of obligation in our children.*

inquire [inkwaiər]   묻다

图 to ask a question

图 ask, enquire, question, investigate, seek

예 *He had to inquire directions several times.*

---

enthusiastic [in θ u:ziǽstik]   열렬한

图 having or showing great excitement and interest

图 zealous, keen, eager, ardent, excited

예 *Enthusiastic crowds filled the streets.*

---

*Vocabulary/Expressions

Day 25

security [sikjúərəti]   안전

图 the state of being free from danger or injury

图 assurance, pledge, protection, safeguard, safety

예 *We support the armed services in the name of national security.*

---

permit [pərmít]   허락하다

图 consent to, give permission

图 admit, allow, enable, grant, let

예 *She permitted her son to visit her estranged husband.*

---

attempt [ətémpt]   시도하다

图 make an effort or attempt

图 assay, effort, endeavor, seek, try

예 *The police attempted to stop the thief.*

---

fierce [fíərs]   사나운, 격렬한

图 marked by extreme and violent energy

图 ferocious, rabid, truculent, violent, vehement

예 *fierce fighting*

---

celebrity [səlebrəti]   유명인사, 명성

图 the state or quality of being widely honored and acclaimed

图 fame, glory, notability, renown, reputation

예 *a Hollywood celebrity*

---

rough [rʌf]   거칠거칠한

图 having or caused by an irregular surface

图 coarse, harsh, ragged, rugged, uneven

예 *rough ground*

desire [dizàiər]   몹시 바라다

뜻 expect and wish

동 hope, trust, want, wish, yearn

예 *I desire she understands that she cannot expect a raise.*

---

miserable [mízərəbl]   비참한

뜻 deserving or inciting pity

동 abject, pitiable, poor, wretched, unhappy

예 *miserable victims of war*

---

estimate [estəmət]   추정하다

뜻 judge tentatively or form an estimate of

동 appraise, compute, evaluate, judge, measure

예 *I estimate this chicken to weigh three pounds.*

---

considerate [kənsídərət]   이해심이 있는

뜻 showing concern for the rights and feelings of others

동 attentive, careful, delicate, heedful, thoughtful

예 *He is considerate enough to leave us alone.*

---

rest [rést]   쉬다

뜻 take a short break from one's activities in order to relax

동 lean, lie, relax, repose, sleep

예 *Rest the dogs for a moment.*

---

duty [djú:ti]   의무

뜻 the social force that binds you to the courses of action demanded by that force

동 assignment, function, obligation, responsibility, undertaking

예 *We must instill a sense of duty in our children.*

---

conspiracy [kənspírəsi]　　　　　　　　　음모

图 a secret agreement between two or more people to perform an unlawful act

동 cabal, collusion, intrigue, plot, scheme

예 *take part in conspiracy*

controlled [kəntróuld]　　　　　　　　억제된

图 restrained or managed or kept within certain bounds

동 composed, disciplined, inhibited, restrained, unflappable

예 *controlled emotions*

necessitate [nəsésətèit]　　　　　　필요로 하다

图 require as useful, just, or proper

동 compel, demand, entail, require, want

예 *This intervention does not necessitate a patient's consent.*

dialogue [daiəlɔ(:)g]　　　　　　　　　대화

图 a conversation between two persons

동 communication, conversation, discourse, speech, talk

예 *I have the dialogue with him.*

haul [hɔːl]　　　　　　　　　세게 잡아당기다

图 draw slowly or heavily

동 cart, drag, hale, pull, trail

예 *haul stones*

repeatedly [ripíːtidli]　　　　　　　되풀이하여

图 several time

동 again and again, frequently, oftentimes, regularly, time after time

예 *It must be washed repeatedly.*

nutrition [nju:tríʃən]　　　　　　　　　　영양
- 图 a source of materials to nourish the body
- 图 alimentation, diet, nourishment, nutriment, sustenance
- 예 *inadequate nutrition*

derive [diràiv]　　　　　　　　　　~을 끌어내다
- 图 be connected by a relationship of blood, for example
- 图 come, descend, get, obtain, originate
- 예 *She was derived from an old Italian noble family.*

skid [skíd]　　　　　　　　　　미끄러지다
- 图 slide without control
- 图 glide, move, slide, slip, slither
- 예 *The car skidded in the curve on the wet road.*

scan [skǽn]　　　　　　　　　　자세히 조사하다
- 图 examine minutely or intensely
- 图 check, examine, investigate, search, survey
- 예 *The surgeon scanned the X-ray.*

pessimistic [pesəmistik]　　　　　　　　비관적인
- 图 expecting the worst possible outcome
- 图 cynical, depressed, distrustful, hopeless, misanthropic
- 예 *take a pessimistic view of*

irrelevant [ireləvənt]　　　　　　　　부적절한
- 图 having no bearing on or connection with the subject at issue
- 图 immaterial, impertinent, irrelative, insignificant, unimportant
- 예 *irrelevant allegations*

visual [víʒuəl]   시각의

图 relating to or using sight

图 discernible, ocular,   optic, optical, visible

예 *visual navigation*

---

unsuspecting [ʌnsəspéktiŋ]   의심하지 않는

图 not suspicious

图 confiding, innocent, trusting, unsuspicious, unwarned

예 *deceiving the unsuspecting public*

---

ongoing [ɔ:ngòuiŋ]   전진, 진행

图 currently happening

图 advancing, continual, continuous, growing, unfinished

예 *an ongoing economic crisis*

---

affect [əfekt]   영향을 미치다

图 have an effect upon

图 impinge, influence, inspire, modify, transform

예 *Will the new rules affect me?*

---

staple [stéipl]   기본적인, 주요한

图 necessary or important, especially regarding food or commodities

图 basic, cardinal, fundamental, major, primary

예 *Wheat is a staple crop.*

---

conductor [kəndʌktər]   지도자

图 the person who leads a musical group

图 director, guard, guide, leader, manager

예 *conductor laureate*

summit [sʌmit]   절정, 정점

图 the highest level or degree attainable

图 acme, apex, top, vertex, zenith

예 *at the summit of his profession*

---

split [split]   쪼개다

图 separate into parts or portions

图 cleave, disjoin, divide, rip, separate

예 *split the cake into three equal parts*

---

outstanding [autstǽndiŋ]   눈에 띄는

图 having a quality that thrusts itself into attention

图 arresting, noticeable, prominent, salient, striking

예 *a outstanding rise in prices*

---

severe [səvíər]   맹렬한

图 very strong or vigorous

图 acute, harsh, strict, strong, violent

예 *strong winds*

---

unfamiliar [ʌnfəmíljər]   익숙치 못한

图 not known or well known

图 new, obscure, strange, unaccustomed, unknown

예 *Be alert at night especially in unfamiliar surroundings.*

---

financial [finǽnʃəl, fai-]   재정의, 재무의

图 involving fiscal matters

图 budgeting, commercial, economic, monetary, pecuniary

예 *financial responsibility*

---

irritate [írətèit]   짜증나게 하다

㊅ cause annoyance in

㊌ annoy, exasperate, nettle, provoke, vex

㊊ *It irritates me that she never closes the door after she leaves.*

celebrity [səlebrəti]   유명인사

㊅ the state or quality of being widely honored and acclaimed

㊌ fame, glory, notability, renown, reputation

㊊ *a Hollywood celebrity*

slide [slàid]   미끄러지다

㊅ move smoothly along a surface

㊌ drift, glide, skid, slip, slither

㊊ *The wheels slid against the sidewalk.*

harmful [háːrmfəl]   유해한

㊅ causing or capable of causing harm

㊌ detrimental, hurtful, injurious, maleficent, noxious

㊊ *harmful effects of smoking*

exclude [iksklúːd]   제외하다

㊅ prevent from being included or considered or accepted

㊌ disallow, eliminate, except, omit, reject

㊊ *The bad results were excluded from the report.*

tease [tíːz]   괴롭히다

㊅ annoy persistently

㊌ annoy, disturb, mock, pester, vex

㊊ *The children teased the boy because of his stammer.*

compete [kəmpíːt] 경쟁하다

图 compete for something

图 contend, contest, emulate, rival, vie

예 *compete against*

---

massive [mǽsiv] 크고 무거운

图 imposing in size or bulk or solidity

图 bulky, large, massy, ponderous, solid

예 *a massive scale*

---

wide [wàid] 폭이 넓은

图 having great extent from one side to the other

图 broad, capacious, extensive, spacious, vast

예 *a river two miles wide*

---

throw [θróu] 던지다

图 place or put with great energy

图 cast, fling, hurl, pitch, toss

예 *thrust the money in the hands of the beggar.*

---

except [iksept] 제외하다

图 prevent from being included or considered or accepted

图 disallow, eliminate, exclude, omit, reject

예 *The bad results were excluded from the report.*

---

promising [prámisiŋ] 장래성 있는

图 full or promise

图 auspicious, bright, hopeful, likely, up-and-coming

예 *a promising new singer on Broadway*

227

concern [kənsɛ́ːrn]   걱정하다

医 be on the mind of

동 bother, occupy, regard, tremble, worry

예 *I concern about the second Germanic consonant shift.*

factual [fǽktʃuəl]   사실의

医 existing in act or fact

동 effective, practical, real, substantial, virtual

예 *the actual things that produced the emotion you experienced*

*Vocabulary/Expressions

Day 26

charm [tʃáːrm] 매혹하다
- 뜻 cause to be enamored
- 동 bewitch, captivate, enchant, fascinate, spellbind
- 예 *She charmed all the men's hearts.*

seemingly [síːminli] 겉으로는
- 뜻 from appearances alone
- 동 apparently, ostensibly, outwardly, professedly, reputedly
- 예 *Seemingly the problem seems minor.*

furnish [fɜːrniʃ] 공급하다
- 뜻 give something useful or necessary to
- 동 endow, provide, purvey, render, supply
- 예 *We furnished the room with an electrical heater.*

pitch [pítʃ] 던지다
- 뜻 throw or toss with a light motion
- 동 cast, flip, throw, shift, toss
- 예 *pitch me newspaper*

tense [téns] 팽팽한
- 뜻 stretched tight
- 동 strained, stretched, taut, tight, uptight
- 예 *tense piano strings*

help [hélp] 돕다
- 뜻 give help or assistance
- 동 aid, assist, relieve, succor, support
- 예 *Everyone helped out during the earthquake.*

enforce [infɔ:rs]　　　　　　　　　　　　　　실시하다

图 compel to behave in a certain way

동 accomplish, apply, begin, compel, impose

예 *Social relations enforce courtesy.*

---

amateur [ǽmət ʃ ùər]　　　　　　　　　　　비 전문가

图 lacking professional skill or expertise

동 amateurish, dabbler, dilettante, inexpert, unskilled

예 *amateur but conscientious efforts*

---

unfair [ʌnfɛ̀ər]　　　　　　　　　　　　　　불공평한

图 marked by injustice or partiality or deception

동 dishonest, inequitable, iniquitous, unjust, wrongful

예 *took an unfair advantage*

---

witness [wítnis]　　　　　　　　　　　　　증명하다

图 be a witness to

동 attest, certify, find, testify, vouch

예 *She witnessed the accident and had to testify in court.*

---

extend [ikstend]　　　　　　　　　　연장하다, 늘이다

图 span an interval of distance, space or time

동 augment, continue, elongate, lengthen, stretch

예 *My land extends over the hills on the horizon.*

---

filter [fíltər]　　　　　　　　　　　　　　여과하다

图 remove by passing through a filter

동 filtrate, infiltrate, leach, percolate, strain

예 *filter out the impurities*

pick [pík]　　　　　　　　　　　　　　　　　골라잡다
- 뜻 select carefully from a group
- 동 choose, cull, gather, pluck, select
- 예 *She finally picked her successor.*

imitate [ímətèit]　　　　　　　　　　　　　　모방하다
- 뜻 reproduce someone's behavior or looks
- 동 copy, counterfeit, mimic, mock, simulate
- 예 *Children often imitate their parents or older siblings.*

comfortable [kʌmftəbl]　　　　　　　　　　　편안한
- 뜻 free from stress or conducive to mental ease
- 동 agreeable, comfy, cozy, easy, snug
- 예 *She's a comfortable person to be with.*

warn [wɔːrn]　　　　　　　　　　　　　　　　경고하다
- 뜻 notify of danger, potential harm, or risk
- 동 acquaint, admonish, advise, caution, remonstrate
- 예 *The director warned him that he might be fired.*

emotional [imóuʃənl]　　　　　　　　　　　감정적인
- 뜻 excessively affected by emotion
- 동 affective, aroused, emotive, sentimental, sensitive
- 예 *He would become emotional over nothing at all.*

branch [bræntʃ]　　　　　　　　　　　　　　부문
- 뜻 a division of some larger or more complex organization
- 동 arm, bureau, category, department, subdivision
- 예 *the Germanic branch of Indo-European languages*

reside [rizàid]　　　　　　　　　　　거주하다
- 图 live in a certain place
- 图 domiciliate, dwell, inhabit, live, occupy
- 예 *She resides in Princeton.*

bright [bràit]　　　　　　　　　　　빛나는
- 图 emitting or reflecting light readily or in large amounts
- 图 brilliant, lucid, radiant, shining, shiny
- 예 *The sun was bright and hot.*

uncomfortable [ʌnkʌmfərtəbl]　　　　거북한
- 图conducive to or feeling mental discomfort;
- 图awkward, comfortless, inconvenient, incommodious, uneasy
- 예 *This kind of life can prove disruptive and uncomfortable.*

unsuitable [ʌnsú:təbl]　　　　　　　부적당한
- 图 not meant or adapted for a particular purpose
- 图 improper, inappropriate, inapt, inexpedient, unfit
- 예 *a solvent unsuitable for use on wood surfaces*

craze [kréiz]　　　　　　　　　　미치게 하다
- 图 cause to go crazy
- 图 bewilder, confuse, distract, frenzy, madden
- 예 *crazed with anger*

statue [stǽt ʃ u:]　　　　　　　　　조각상
- 图 a sculpture representing a human or animal
- 图 figure, icon, image, sculpture, statuary
- 예 *plan a statue in one's honor*

enroll [inróul]　　　　　　　　　　　　등록하다
- register formally as a participant or member
- enlist, enrol, enter, inscribe, recruit
- *The party enrolled many new members.*

oppose [əpouz]　　　　　　　　　　　　반대하다
- express opposition to
- dissent, object, resist, thwart, withstand
- *We oppose the ban on abortion.*

accept [æksépt]　　　　　　　　　　　　받아들이다
- receive willingly something given or offered
- admit, allow, receive, recognize, take
- *I won't accept this dog in my house.*

spot [spát]　　　　　　　　　　　　　　반점
- a blemish made by dirt
- blot, dot, fleck, speck, stain
- *He had a spot on his cheek.*

relevance [réləvəns]　　　　　　　　적절, 타당성
- the relation of something to the matter at hand
- applicability, concernment, materiality, pertinence, relevancy
- *have relevance to*

delicious [dilíʃəs]　　　　　　　　　　맛있는
- extremely pleasing to the sense of taste
- delectable, luscious, sapid, toothsome, yummy
- *a delicious dinner*

prove [prú:v]   입증하다

医 establish the validity of something, as by an example, explanation or experiment

同 attest, demonstrate, establish, show, substantiate

예 *The experiment proved the instability of the compound.*

---

removal [rimú:vəl]   제거

医 the act of removing

同 banishment, elimination, eradication, remotion, transference

예 *He had surgery for the removal of a malignancy.*

---

exchange [ikstʃeindʒ]   교환하다, 환전하다

医 the act of changing one thing for another thing

同 change, interchange, reciprocate, replace, trade

예 *Adam was promised immortality in exchange for his disobedience.*

---

constant [kánstənt]   불변의

医 uninterrupted in time and indefinitely long continuing

同 ceaseless, incessant, perpetual, unceasing, unremitting

예 *in constant pain*

---

mischief [místʃif]   해악

医 reckless or malicious behavior that causes discomfort or annoyance in others

同 damage, evil, harm, injury, prank

예 *get up to mischief*

---

injure [índʒər]   상처를 입히다

医 cause injuries or bodily harm to

同 bruise, hurt, offend, spite, wound

예 *She injure me when she did not include me among her guests.*

---

adopt [ədápt]   채택하다

图 take on a certain form, attribute, or aspect

图 assume, acquire, embrace, ratify, take

예 *He adopted an air of superiority.*

---

perceive [pərsí:v]   지각하다

图 to become aware of through the senses

图 comprehend, discern, notice, realize, see

예 *I could perceive the ship coming over the horizon.*

---

executive [igzekjutiv]   임원

图 a person responsible for the administration of a business

图 administrator, chief, director, manager, officer

예 *a business executive*

---

director [diréktər]   지도자

图 someone who controls resources and expenditures

图 conductor, governor, head, leader, manager

예 *managing director*

---

quantity [kwántəti]   양

图 how much there is or how many there are of something that you can quantify

图 amount, measure, number, quantum, volume

예 *a negligible quantity*

---

shape [ʃéip]   모양

图 the spatial arrangement of something as distinct from its substance

图 appearance, condition, figure, form, mold

예 *Geometry is the mathematical science of shape.*

---

grateful [gréitfəl] 감사하는
图 feeling or showing gratitude
图 appreciative, beholden, obliged, pleased, thankful
예 *a grateful heart*

violence [vàiələns] 격렬
图 the property of being wild or turbulent
图 ferocity, fierceness, outrage, severity, vehemence
예 *the storm's violence*

liberal [líbərəl] 관대한
图 showing or characterized by broad-mindedness
图 benevolent, bounteous, bountiful, generous, tolerant
예 *generous and broad sympathies*

pain [péin] 아픔, 고통
图 a symptom of some physical hurt or disorder
图 ache, affliction, grief, misery, suffering
예 *The patient developed severe pain and distension.*

shorten [ʃɔːrtn] 짧게하다
图 make shorter than originally intended
图 abbreviate, abridge, curtail, cut, reduce
예 *He shortened his trip due to illness.*

glance [glǽns] 흘긋 보다, 잠깐 보다
图 take a brief look at
图 browse, glint, peek, peep, peer
예 *She only glanced at the paper.*

fancy [fǽnsi] 공상하다

图 see in one's mind

图 conceive, imagine, like, suppose, think

예 *I can fancy what will happen.*

---

sanitation [sæ nətei ʃ ən] 위생

图 the state of being clean and conducive to health

图 asepsis, cleanliness, disinfection, hygiene, hygienics

예 *urban sanitation*

---

crude [kru:d]   천연 그대로의, 가공하지 않은

뜻 not processed or subjected to analysis

동 homemade, natural, raw, unprocessed, unworked

예 *crude data*

---

session [seʃən]   개회, 회의

뜻 a meeting for execution of a group's functions

동 assembly, concourse, conference, gathering, sitting

예 *It was the opening session of the legislature.*

---

equilibrium [ìːkwəlíbriəm]   평형

뜻 equality of distribution

동 balance, counterpoise, poise, equilibration, equipoise

예 *equilibrium point*

---

shock [ʃák]   충격을 주다

뜻 knock someone's socks off

동 flabbergast, horrify, scandalize, shake, startle

예 *I was shocked when I heard that I was promoted.*

---

creative [kriéitiv]   창조적인

뜻 having the ability or power to create

동 imaginative, innovative, originative, productive, stimulating

예 *a creative imagination*

---

stun [stʌn]   아연하게 하다

뜻 overcome as with astonishment or disbelief

동 bemuse, deafen, dumbfound, stagger, stupefy

예 *The news stunned her.*

---

embarrass [imbǽrəs]　　　　　　　　　　어리둥절하게 하다

㊄ cause to be embarrassed

㊌ confuse, disconcert, nonplus, perplex, puzzle

㊀ *embarrass a person with questions*

---

pray [préi]　　　　　　　　　　　　　　간청하다

㊄ call upon in supplication

㊌ beg, entreat, implore, request, supplicate

㊀ *I pray you to stop!*

---

classify [klǽsəfai]　　　　　　　　　　분류하다

㊄ arrange or order by classes or categories

㊄ assort, categorize, class, separate, sort

㊀ *How would you classify these pottery shards?*

---

impatient [impeiʃənt]　　　　　　　　조급한, 참을성 없는

㊄ restless or short-tempered under delay or opposition

㊌ hasty, intolerant, irascible, irritable, restive

㊀ *impatient of criticism*

---

define [difàin]　　　　　　　　　　　뜻을 명확히 하다

㊄ decide upon or fix definitely

㊌ determine, fix, limit, set, specify

㊀ *define the parameters*

---

predict [pridíkt]　　　　　　　　　　예언하다

㊄ make a prediction about

㊌ anticipate, forebode, foretell, presage, prognosticate

㊀ *predict the outcome of an election.*

learn [lɛ:rn]　　　　　　　　　　　　　　　　　배우다
- 图 gain knowledge or skills
- 图 acquire, larn, read, study, teach
- 例 *She learned dancing from her sister.*

recognition [rekəgniʃən]　　　　　　　인식, 인정, 인지
- 图 the state or quality of being recognized or acknowledged
- 图 admission, awareness, consciousness, noticing, realization
- 例 *The partners were delighted with the recognition of their work.*

circle [sɛ:rkl]　　　　　　　　　　　　　　선회하다
- 图 move in circles
- 图 begird, compass, revolve, surround, wheel
- 例 *come full circle*

contemporary [kəntempəreri]　　　　　　같은 시대의
- 图 characteristic of the present
- 图 coeval, current, modern-day, present, up-to-date
- 例 *contemporary trends in design*

quotation [kwoutéiʃən]　　　　　　　　　　　인용
- 图 a short note recognizing a source of information or of a quoted passage
- 图 acknowledgment, citation, mention, quote, reference
- 例 *The quotations are usually printed at the front of a book.*

pupil [pjú:pəl]　　　　　　　　　　　　　　　학생
- 图 a learner who is enrolled in an educational institution
- 图 apprentice, disciple, learner, schoolboy, student
- 例 *pupils´ products*

muse [mjúːz]   묵상하다
- 图 reflect deeply on a subject
- 图 contemplate, meditate, ponder, ruminate, think
- 예 *I mused the events of the afternoon.*

propose [prəpóuz]   제안하다
- 图 make a proposal, declare a plan for something
- 图 advise, intend, offer, propound, suggest
- 예 *The senator proposed to abolish the sales tax.*

magnificent [mægnífəsnt]   웅장한
- 图 characterized by or attended with brilliance or grandeur
- 图 gorgeous, grand, majestic, palatial, splendid
- 예 *magnificent cathedrals*

spoil [spɔil]   망치다
- 图 make a mess of, destroy or ruin
- 图 botch, destroy, fumble, ruin, vitiate
- 예 *I spoiled the dinner and we had to eat out.*

exceed [iksíːd]   ~의 한도를 넘다
- 图 be or do something to a greater degree
- 图 excel, outdo, surpass, transcend, transgress
- 예 *This exceeds all my expectations.*

rough [rʌf]   거칠거칠한
- 图 having or caused by an irregular surface
- 图 coarse, harsh, ragged, rugged, uneven
- 예 *rough ground*

solve [sálv]   풀다
- 医 find the solution to or understand the meaning of
- 동 answer, decide, elucidate, settle, unravel
- 예 *Did you solve the problem?*

indeed [indíːd]   참으로
- 医 in truth often tends to intensify
- 동 actually, in fact, really, truly, verily
- 예 *They said the car would break down and indeed it did.*

delight [dilàit]   매우 기뻐하다
- 医 give pleasure to or be pleasing to
- 동 enjoy, gladden, please, rejoice, revel
- 예 *He delights in his granddaughter.*

sorrowful [sárəfəl]   슬퍼하는
- 医 experiencing or marked by or expressing sorrow especially that associated with irreparable loss
- 동 doleful, lugubrious, mournful, sad, woeful
- 예 *sorrowful news*

mention [ménʃən]   언급하다
- 医 make reference to
- 동 advert, cite, note, observe, remark
- 예 *His name was mentioned in connection with the invention.*

select [silékt]   고르다
- 医 pick out, select, or choose from a number of alternatives
- 동 choose, cull, opt, pick, take
- 예 *She selected a pair of shoes from among the dozen the salesgirl had shown her.*

inactive [inǽktiv]   나태한, 피동적인
图 lacking in energy or will
图 indolent, inert, passive, sluggish, torpid
예 *an inactive membe*

echo [ékou]   반향하다
图 ring or echo with sound
图 repeat, resound, reverberate, ring, sound
예 *The hall resounded with laughter.*

rescue [réskju:]   구출하다
图 free from harm or evil
图 redeem, retrieve, salvage, salve, save
예 *rescue a sunken ship*

foretell [fɔːrtél]   예고하다
图 make a prediction about
图 anticipate, forebode, foresee, predict, prognosticate
예 *foretell the outcome of an election*

primitive [prímətiv]   원시의
图 belonging to an early stage of technical development
图 aboriginal, original, primaeval, primeval, pristine
예 *primitive movies of the 1890s*

definitely [défənitli]   명확히
图 without question and beyond doubt
图 absolutely, certainly, decidedly, positively, surely
예 *It was definitely too expensive.*

hardly [háːrdli]   거의~않다

㊀ almost not

㊀ infrequently, rarely, scarcely, seldom, uncommonly

㊀ *He hardly ever goes fishing.*

ethical [éθikəl]   윤리적인

㊀ adhering to ethical and moral principles

㊀ conscientious, humane, moral, righteous, virtuous

㊀ *It seems ethical and right.*

recruit [rikrúːt]   모집하다

㊀ register formally as a participant or member

㊀ enlist, enrol, enroll, enter, inscribe

㊀ *The party recruited many new members.*

destroy [distrɔ́i]   파괴하다

㊀ do away with, cause the destruction or undoing of

㊀ annihilate, demolish, ruin, spoil, wreck

㊀ *The fire destroyed the house.*

regret [rigrét]   후회하다

㊀ feel remorse for

㊀ deplore, grieve, mourn, repent, rue

㊀ *I regret to say that you did not gain admission to Harvard.*

possibly [pásəbli]   아마

㊀ by chance

㊀ maybe, peradventure, perchance, perhaps, probably

㊀ *Possibly she will call tomorrow.*

rational [ræ∫ənl]   이성적인

图 consistent with or based on or using reason

图 intellectual, logical, reasonable, sane, sensible

예 *rational behavior*

---

conviction [kənvík∫ən]   확신

图 an unshakable belief in something without need for proof or evidence

图 belief, confidence, faith, opinion, persuasion

예 *a conviction about*

---

nonetheless [nʌnðəlés]   그럼에도 불구하고

图 despite anything to the contrary

图 nevertheless, notwithstanding, still, though, yet

예 *He was a stern nonetheless fair master.*

---

capacity [kəpǽsəti]   재능

图 capability to perform or produce

图 ability, capability, competence, power, talent

예 *a great capacity for growth*

---

swallow [swálou]   삼키다, 들이키다

图 pass through the esophagus as part of eating or drinking

图 devour, drink, engulf, gulp, ingest

예 *Swallow the raw fish--it won't kill you!*

---

wrap [ræp]   싸다

图 arrange or fold as a cover or protection

图 cover, envelop, muffle, pack, swathe

예 *Wrap the present.*

Day 27

humble [hʌmbl] 겸손한

톙 marked by meekness or modesty

쵍 biddable, lowly, modest, sedate, unassuming

옣 *a humble apology*

alternative [ɔːltɛːrnətiv] 대안

톙 one of a number of things from which only one can be chosen

쵍 choice, option, pick, redundancy, selection

옣 *What alternative did I have?*

*Vocabulary/Expressions

associate [əsouʃieit] 연상하다
- 뜻 make a logical or causal connection
- 동 combine, connect, correlate, link, relate
- 예 *I cannot associate these two pieces of evidence in my mind.*

---

awkwardly [ɔːkwərdli] 어색하게
- 뜻 not easily managed or effected
- 동 bunglingly, clumsily, gracelessly, ineptly, unskillfully
- 예 *He bent awkwardly.*

---

species [spíːʃiːz] 종
- 뜻 a specific kind of something
- 동 class, genus, kind, sort, type
- 예 *a species of molecule*

---

perform [pərfɔːrm] 이행하다, 실행하다
- 뜻 carry out or perform an action
- 동 accomplish, act, discharge, execute, fulfill
- 예 *John performed the painting, the weeding, and he cleaned out the gutters.*

---

humble [hʌmbl] 겸손한
- 뜻 marked by meekness or modesty
- 동 biddable, lowly, modest, sedate, unassuming
- 예 *a humble apology*

---

simply [símpli] 다만
- 뜻 and nothing more
- 동 but, just, merely, only, plainly
- 예 *I was merely asking.*

---

detect [ditekt] 발견하다

图 discover or determine the existence, presence, or fact of

图 discover, find, notice, observe, uncover

예 *She detected high levels of lead in her drinking water.*

defeat [difí:t] 쳐부수다, 패배시키다

图 win a victory over

图 beat, conquer, overcome, overpower, vanquish

예 *Defeat your enemies.*

attraction [ətrǽkʃən] 매력

图 the quality of arousing interest

图 allurement, charm, fascination, magnetism, seduction

예 *Her personality held a strange attraction for him.*

invaluable [invǽljuəbl] 매우 귀중한

图 having incalculable monetary, intellectual, or spiritual worth

图 *costly, priceless, inestimable, inappreciable, precious*

예 *invaluable help*

depict [dipíkt] 묘사하다

图 show in, or as in, a picture

图 describe, draw, limn, picture, portray

예 *This scene depicts country life.*

subtract [səbtrǽkt] ~에서 빼다

图 take off or away

图 abstract, deduct, detract, withdraw, withhold

예 *Subtract this amount from my paycheck.*

depend [dipénd]   의존하다

図 have faith or confidence in

동 count, entrust, hope, lean, rely

예 *Depend on your family in times of crisis.*

---

haste [héist]   급함

図 a condition of urgency making it necessary to hurry

동 hurry, hustle, nimbleness, promptness, swiftness

예 *in a haste to lock the door*

---

move [mú:v]   움직이다

図 change location

동 budge, go, locomote, stir, travel

예 *The soldiers moved towards the city in an attempt to take it before night fell.*

---

sculpture [skʌlptʃər]   조각하다

図 create by shaping stone or wood or any other hard material

동 carve, chisel, engrave, model, sculpt

예 *Sculpture a swan out of a block of ice.*

---

bring [bríŋ]   가져오다

図 go or come after and bring or take back

동 carry, convey, fetch, get, take

예 *Could you bring the wine?*

---

commute [kəmjú:t]   교환하다

図 exchange positions without a change in value

동 change, exchange, switch, trade, transpose

예 *These operators commute with each other.*

---

exercise [éksərsàiz]
연습시키다

图 give a workout to

동 drill, exert, practice, train, wield

예 *This puzzle will exercise your mind.*

senior [síːnjər]
손위의

图 advanced in years

동 aged, elderly, major, older, superior

예 *senior members of the society*

ancient [éinʃənt]
먼 옛날의

图 belonging to times long past

동 antiquity, archaic, old, olden, primitive

예 *ancient history*

entertain [èntərtéin]
즐겁게 하다

图 provide entertainment for

동 amuse, cheer, divert, gratify, please

예 *entertain guests*

broadcast [brɔːdkæst]
(소문을) 퍼뜨리다

图 cause to become widely known

동 diffuse, disseminate, propagate, spread, transmit

예 *broadcast information*

seriousness [síəriəsnis]
진지함, 중대함

图 the trait of being serious

동 earnestness, gravity, magnitude, sincerity, worth

예 *a lack of seriousness*

intensity [inténsəti]   강도

图 the amount of energy transmitted

图 force, intension, power, strength, violence

예 *He adjusted the intensity of the sound.*

---

release [rili:s]   발표하다

图 prepare and issue for public distribution or sale

图 free, issue, notice, publish, unbind

예 *Release a magazine or newspaper.*

---

merry [méri]   명량한, 유쾌한

图 offering fun and gaiety

图 festal, festive, gay, jocund, mirthful

예 *merry and exciting night life*

---

convenient [kənví:njənt]   편리한

图 suited to your comfort or purpose or needs

图 appropriate, comfortable, fit, opportune, suitable

예 *a convenient excuse for not going*

---

attendant [əténdənt]   부수적인

图 following or accompanying as a consequence

图 accompanying, concomitant, consequent, ensuant, incidental

예 *attendant circumstances*

---

abundance [əbʌndəns]   풍부

图 the property of a more than adequate quantity or supply

图 affluence, copiousness, opulence, plenty, teemingness

예 *an age of abundance*

sequence [síːkwəns]   연달아 일어남, 연속

图 serial arrangement in which things follow in logical order or a recurrent
pattern

图 continuance, order, sequel, series, succession

예 *The sequence of names was alphabetical.*

---

intensify [inténsəfài]   세게 하다

图 make more intense, stronger, or more marked

图 amplify, enhance, increase, reinforce, strengthen

예 *The efforts were intensified.*

---

consist [kənsíst]   이루어져 있다

图 be composed of

图 compose, comprise, constitute, make up, relate

예 *What does this dish consist of?*

---

custom [kʌ́stəm]   습관

图 accepted or habitual practice

图 addiction, consuetude, habit, praxis, usage

예 *Custom is second nature.*

---

rid [ríd]   자유롭게 하다

图 relieve from

图 free, liberate, redeem, release, relieve

예 *Rid the house of pests.*

---

cite [sàit]   인용하다

图 make reference to

图 adduce, mention, quote, refer, summon

예 *His name was cited in connection with the invention.*

---

static [stǽtik]　　　　　　　　　　　　　　　　　　　　　정적인

图 not in physical motion

동 changeless, inactive, motionless, stationary, still

예 *the static of an object at rest*

---

despair [dispɛ̀ər]　　　　　　　　　　　　　　　　　　　절망

图 a state in which all hope is lost or absent

동 anguish, desperation, despondency, hopelessness, tribulation

예 *in the depths of despair*

---

exhausted [igzɔ́:stid]　　　　　　　　　　　　　　　　다 써버린

图 drained of energy or effectiveness

동 fatigued, spent, tired, weary, worn-out

예 *I felt completely exhausted*

---

present [préznt]　　　　　　　　　　　　　　　　　　증정하다

图 give as a present

동 award, donate, furnish, give, offer

예 *What will you present her for her birthday?*

---

prevalence [prévələns]　　　　　　　　　　　　　　　유행

图 being widespread

동 currency, popularity, predominance, ubiquity, vogue

예 *He was surprised by the prevalence of optimism about the future.*

---

destruction [distrʌkʃən]　　　　　　　　　　　　　　파괴

图 the termination of something by causing so much damage to it that it cannot be repaired or no longer exists

동 annihilation, devastation, ravage, ruination, wreck

예 *widespread destruction*

further [fɛ:rðər]   게다가

囿 in addition or furthermore

同 besides, farther, furthermore. more. moreover

例 *Stated further that he would not cooperate with them.*

---

permission [pərmíʃən]   허가

囿 approval to do something

同 acceptance, allowance, concession, sanction, warrant

例 *He asked permission to leave.*

---

supplement [sʌpləmənt]   추가

囿 a quantity added

同 addition, appendix, complement, extra, subsidiary

例 *supplement a budget*

---

across [əkrɔ:s]   가로질러

囿 to the opposite side

同 athwart, crossways, crosswise, over, transversely

例 *The football field was 300 feet across.*

---

judgment [dʒʌdʒmənt]   판단

囿 an opinion formed by judging something

同 decision, judgement, opinion, sentence, verdict

例 *He was reluctant to make his judgment known.*

---

construct [kənstrʌkt]   건설하다, 조립하다

囿 make by combining materials and parts

同 build, erect, form, frame, make

例 *Some eccentric constructed an electric brassiere warmer.*

---

operate [ápəreit]   작용하다

🈂 perform as expected when applied

🈹 act, function, go, run, work

🈸 *The washing machine won't operate unless it's plugged in.*

---

approximately [əpráksəmətli]   대략

🈂 imprecise but fairly close to correct

🈹 about, around, nearly, roughly, thereabouts

🈸 *It lasted approximately an hour.*

---

*Vocabulary/Expressions

---

aggressive [əgrésiv]   공격적인

㈜ characteristic of an enemy or one eager to fight

⑧ belligerent, contentious, hostile, offensive, truculent

㈁ *aggressive acts against another country*

---

hire [hàiər]   고용하다

㈜ engage or hire for work

⑧ apply, employ, engage, use, utilize

㈁ *They hired two new secretaries in the department.*

---

surface [sə́ːrfis]   표면

㈜ the outer boundary of an artifact or a material layer constituting or resembling such a boundary

⑧ covering, exterior, external, exterior, superficial

㈁ *The cloth had a pattern of red dots on a white surface.*

---

various [vɛ̀əriəs]   가지각색의

㈜ of many different kinds purposefully arranged but lacking any uniformity

⑧ assorted, different, manifold, sundry, varied

㈁ *His disguises are many and various.*

---

scandal [skǽndl]   추문

㈜ disgraceful gossip about the private lives of other people

⑧ detraction, disgrace, gossip, shame, slander

㈁ *a political scandal*

---

punctual [pʌ́ŋktʃuəl]   시간을 잘 지키는

㈜ acting or arriving or performed exactly at the time appointed

⑧ appropriate, fitting, opportune, seasonable, timely

㈁ *She expected guests to be punctual at meals.*

---

play [pléi]　　　　　　　　　　　　　　　　　　놀다

图 participate in games or sport

图 act, gambol, perform, rejoice, toy

예 *We played hockey all afternoon.*

---

satisfaction [sæ tisfǽk ʃ ən]　　　　　　　만족

图 state of being gratified or satisfied

图 achievement, complacency, contentment, fulfillment, gratification

예 *Dull repetitious work gives no satisfaction.*

---

tight [tàit]　　　　　　　　　　　　　　　　단단한

图 closely constrained or constricted or constricting

图 close, narrow, taut, tense, unyielding

예 *He hated tight starched collars.*

---

mutual [mjuːt ʃ uəl]　　　　　　　　　　　　공통의

图 common to or shared by two or more parties

图 common, communal, intermutual, public, shared

예 *the mutual interests of management and labor*

---

decision [disíʒən]　　　　　　　　　　　　　결정

图 a position or opinion or judgment reached after consideration

图 conclusion, determination, finding, ruling, verdict

예 *a decision unfavorable to the opposition*

---

suspect [səspekt]　　　　　　　　　　　　　짐작하다

图 imagine to be the case or true or probable

图 doubt, guess, misdoubt, presume, reckon

예 *I suspect he is a fugitive.*

---

flash [flǽʃ]   번쩍거리게 하다

图 gleam or glow intermittently

图 blink, glitter, sparkle, twinkle, winkle

예 *The lights were flashing.*

---

outward [àutwərd]   외부의

图 toward the outside

图 exterior, external, outdoor, outer, outside

예 *Move the needle further outward.*

---

target [tá:rgit]   과녁, 목표

图 the goal intended to be attained

图 aim, goal, object, mark, purpose

예 *The sole object of her trip was to see her children.*

---

weak [wí:k]   약한

图 wanting in physical strength

图 debilitated, feeble, frail, infirm, weakly

예 *a weak pillar*

---

emergency [imɛ́:rdʒənsi]   비상사태

图 a sudden unforeseen crisis that requires immediate action

图 crisis, danger, exigency, predicament, urgency

예 *He never knew what to do in an emergency.*

---

acknowledge [æknálidʒ]   인정하다

图 declare to be true or admit the existence or reality or truth of

图 avow, concede, confess, endorse, recognize

예 *She acknowledged that she might have forgotten.*

moist [mɔist]   축축한
- 图 slightly wet
- 图 damp, dank, humid, soggy, wet
- 예 *clothes moist with perspiration*

numerous [njuːmərəs] .   다수의, 셀 수 없이 많은
- 图 amounting to a large indefinite number
- 图 many, infinite, multitudinous, legion, plentiful
- 예 *numerous times*

compel [kəmpel]   강요하다
- 图 force somebody to do something
- 图 constrain, enforce, force, impel, oblige
- 예 *The water shortage compels conservation.*

tremendous [trimendəs]   거대한
- 图 extraordinarily large in size or extent or amount or power or degree
- 图 colossal, enormous, huge, monstrous, vast
- 예 *A plane took off with a tremendous noise.*

decentralize [diːsentrəlaiz]   분산시키다
- 图 make less central
- 图 deconcentrate, diffract, disject, dispersion, separate
- 예 *After the revolution, food distribution was decentralized.*

integral [íntigrəl]   절대 필요한
- 图 existing as an essential constituent or characteristic
- 图 complete, essential, fundamental, indispensable, necessary
- 예 *a integral inability to tell the truth*

area [ɛ́əriə] 지역

㈜ a particular geographical region of indefinite boundary

㈜ district, field, region, territory, zone

㈜ *It was a mountainous area.*

free [fríː] 자유롭게 하다

㈜ remove or force out from a position

㈜ dislodge, emancipate, liberate, release, relieve

㈜ *He finally could free the legs of the earthquake victim who was buried in the rubble.*

unprepared [ʌnpripɛ́ərd] 준비 없는, 즉석의

㈜ without preparation

㈜ extemporaneous, extempore, impromptu, unplanned, unready

㈜ *unprepared remarks*

flattery [flǽtəri] 아첨

㈜ excessive or insincere praise

㈜ adulation, blandishment, compliment, palaver, sycophancy

㈜ *inane flattery*

product [prádʌkt] 생산품

㈜ commodities offered for sale

㈜ commodity, manufacture, merchandise, output, ware

㈜ *Good business depends on having good product.*

deficit [défəsit] 부족

㈜ the property of being an amount by which something is less than expected or required

㈜ deficiency, insufficiency, paucity, scantiness, shortage

㈜ *make up a deficit*

complement [kámpləmənt] 보완하는것

- 뜻 something added to complete or embellish or make perfect
- 동 addition, accompaniment, adjunct, enhancement, supplement
- 예 *A fine wine is a perfect complement to the dinner.*

await [əwéit] 기다리다, 대기하다

- 뜻 look forward to the probable occurrence of
- 동 anticipate, bide, expect, wait, watch
- 예 *He is waiting to be drafted.*

familiar [fəmíljər] 잘 알려진

- 뜻 well known or easily recognized
- 동 accustomed, acquainted, close, conversant, intimate
- 예 *a familiar figure*

primarily [praimérəli] 첫째로

- 뜻 of primary import
- 동 chiefly, first, mainly, originally, principally
- 예 *This is primarily a question of economics.*

lore [lɔːr] 지식

- 뜻 knowledge gained through tradition or anecdote
- 동 erudition, knowledge, learning, science, tale
- 예 *Early peoples passed on plant and animal lore through legend.*

abrupt [əbrʌpt] 갑작스러운, 뜻밖의

- 뜻 exceedingly sudden and unexpected
- 동 hurried, jerky, surprising, unexpected, unforeseen
- 예 *an abrupt change in the weather*

deposit [dipázit]
두다

- 图 put something somewhere firmly
- 圄 locate, lodge, lay, place, settle
- 例 *Deposit the suitcase on the bench.*

---

stressful [strésfəl]
긴장이 많은

- 图 extremely irritating to the nerves
- 圄 annoying, distressing, irritating, maddening, upsetting
- 例 *the stressful days before a war*

---

punish [pʌniʃ]
벌하다

- 图 impose a penalty on
- 圄 amerce, castigate, chasten, discipline, penalize
- 例 *We had to punish the dog for soiling the floor again.*

---

skeptical [sképtikəl]
의심많은, 회의적인

- 图 marked by or given to doubt
- 圄 doubting, incredulous, questioning, sceptical, suspicious
- 例 *a skeptical listener*

---

interrupt [intərʌpt]
방해하다

- 图 interfere in someone else's activity
- 圄 discontinue, disturb, impede, intercept, interfere
- 例 *Please don't interrupt me while I'm on the phone.*

---

moral [mɔːrəl]
도덕의

- 图 concerned with principles of right and wrong or conforming to standards of behavior and character based on those principles
- 圄 ethic, ethical, innocent, righteous, virtuous
- 例 *moral sense*

---

surveil [sərvéil]   감시하다

图 keep under surveillance

图 follow, observe, oversee, survey, watch

예 *surveil the enemy*

---

earn [ə :rn]   벌다, 획득하다

图 acquire or deserve by one's efforts or actions

图 acquire, gain, make, merit, win

예 *She earns a lot in her new job.*

---

slam [slǽm]   탕 닫다

图 close violently

图 bang, crash, hit, strike, swat

예 *He slammed the door shut.*

---

follow [fálou]   ...의 뒤를 잇다

图 to travel behind, go after, come after

图 attend, ensue, go after, pursue, succeed

예 *Please follow the guide through the museum.*

---

replace [ripleis]   교체하다

图 substitute a person or thing for

图 alter, change, displace, substitute, supersede

예 *He replaced the old razor blade.*

---

roar [rɔːr]   고함치

图 make a loud noise, as of wind, water, or vehicles

图 bellow, howl, rumble, shout, yell

예 *The water roared down the chute.*

---

recite [risàit]   암송하다

囿 repeat aloud from memory

톱 declaim, narrate, recount, speak, tell

예 *She recited a poem.*

incredible [inkredəbl]   놀라운

囿 beyond belief or understanding

톱 fabulous, improbable, inconceivable, unbelievable, unlikely

예 *The book's plot is simply incredible.*

*Vocabulary/Expressions

immediate [imi:diət]   즉각의
- 图 very close or connected in space or time
- 图 direct, instant, instantaneous, prompt, proximate
- 例 *immediate contact*

---

convention [kənven ʃən]   집회
- 图 a large formal assembly
- 图 assembly, covenant, conference, meeting, treaty
- 例 *political convention*

---

darken [dá:rkən]   어둡게하다, 희미하게 하다
- 图 become dark or darker
- 图 cloud, dim, obscure, overcast, shade
- 例 *The sky darkened.*

---

enlightenment [inlàitnmənt]   계발, 교화
- 图 education that results in understanding and the spread of knowledge
- 图 awareness, civilization, education, refinement, understanding
- 例 *the age of enlightenment*

---

undergo [ʌndərgou]   겪다
- 图 pass through
- 图 confront, experience, face, front, meet
- 例 *undergo a strange sensation*

---

determine [ditə :rmin]   결정하다
- 图 reach, make, or come to a decision about something
- 图 conclude, decide, fix, resolve, settle
- 例 *We finally determined after lengthy deliberations.*

---

location [loukéiʃən]　　　　　　　　　　위치

图 a determination of the place where something is

동 locality, place, position, site, spot

예 *He got a good location on the target.*

---

prevail [priveil]　　　　　　　　　　우세하다

图 be larger in number, quantity, power, status or importance

동 dominate, influence, overcome, predominate, preponderate

예 *Hispanics prevail in this neighborhood.*

---

typical [típikəl]　　　　　　　　　　전형적인

图 exhibiting the qualities or characteristics that identify a group or kind or category

동 conventional, exemplary, general, quintessential, usual

예 *a typical case of arteritis*

---

relatively [rélətivli]　　　　　　　　　상대적으로

图 by comparison to something else

동 approximately, comparatively, proportionately, rather, somewhat

예 *The situation is relatively calm now.*

---

contend [kəntend]　　　　　　　　　　싸우다

图 be engaged in a fight

동 combat, contest, fight, grapple, struggle

예 *Militant groups are contending for control of the country.*

---

nutritious [njutríʃəs]　　　　　　　　영양이 되는

图 of or providing nourishment

동 alimental, alimentary, nourishing, nutrient, nutritive

예 *good nourishing stew*

---

recommend [rekəmend]   추천하다

圏 push for something

圄 advise, commend, counsel, suggest, urge

예 *The travel agent recommended strongly that we not travel on Thanksgiving Day.*

---

point [pɔint]   가리키다

圏 indicate a place, direction, person, or thing

圄 denote, designate, indicate, show, signify

예 *He pointed to the empty parking space.*

---

conscience [kánʃəns]   양심

圏 a feeling of shame when you do something immoral

圄 consciousness, duty, mind, morals, scruples

예 *He has no conscience about his cruelty.*

---

rely [rilài]   의지하다

圏 have confidence or faith in

圄 confide, depend, lean, swear, trust

예 *Rely on your friends.*

---

anxious [ǽŋkʃəs]   걱정하는

圏 causing or fraught with or showing anxiety

圄 nervous, restless, solicitous, uneasy, worried

예 *She cast anxious glances behind her*

---

accurate [ǽkjurət]   정확한

圏 conforming exactly or almost exactly to fact or to a standard or performing with total accuracy

圄 correct, exact, precise, right, true

예 *an accurate reproduction*

Day 30

merit [merit]   장점

㈜ any admirable quality or attribute

⑧ advantage, virtue, excellence, strong point, excellence

㈖ *work of great merit*

---

article [ɑ́:rtikl]   물품

㈜ nonfictional prose forming an independent part of a publication

⑧ commodity, item, object, section, thing

㈖ *in the article of*

---

lead [lí:d]   인도하다

㈜ take somebody somewhere

⑧ conduct, direct, drive, guide, take

㈖ *We lead him to our chief.*

---

educated [édʒukèitid]   교육받은

㈜ possessing an education especially having more than average knowledge

⑧ cultivated, enlightened, learned, lettered, trained

㈖ *an enlightened electorate*

---

carve [kɑ́:rv]   새기다

㈜ engrave or cut by chipping away at a surface

⑧ chisel, engrave, incise, sculpture, slice

㈖ *carve one's name into the bark*

---

interest [íntərəst]   관심, 흥미

㈜ a sense of concern with and curiosity about someone or something

⑧ attention, concern, curiosity, notice, preoccupation

㈖ *an interest in music*

seldom [séldəm]   드물게

图 not often

图 hardly, infrequently, occasionally, rarely, uncommonly

예 *We rarely met.*

---

extraordinary [ikstrɔːrdənèri]   비상한

图 beyond what is ordinary or usual

图 exceptional, odd, remarkable, special, unusual

예 *her extraordinary beauty*

---

beforehand [bifɔːrhænd]   미리, 벌써

图 ahead of time

图 ahead, early, fore, in advance, previously

예 *We like to plan beforehand.*

---

irresistible [irizístəbl]   저항할 수 없는

图 impossible to resist

图 compelling, inescapable, overpowering, overwhelming, resistless

예 *What happens when an irresistible force meets an immovable object?*

---

wealthy [wélθi]   부유한

图having an abundant supply of money or possessions of value

图 affluent, moneyed, opulent, prosperous, rich

예*wealthy corporations*

---

uninterrupted [ʌnìntərʌptid]   연속

图 continuing in time or space without interruption

图 ceaseless, continuous, incessant, unceasing, unremitting

예 *He lived in uninterrupted fear.*

inform [infɔ:rm]   알리다

图 impart knowledge of some fact, state or affairs, or event to

동 announce, apprise, notify, report, tell

예 *I informed him of his rights*

---

instinctive [instíŋktiv]   본능적인

图 prompted by (or as if by) instinct

동 automatic, innate, intrinsic, natural, spontaneous

예 *a cat's instinctive aversion to water*

---

communicate [kəmjú:nəkèit]   전달하다

图 transmit information

동 convey, impart, inform, suggest, transmit

예 *Please communicate this message to all employees.*

---

healing [hí:liŋ]   치료하는

图 tending to cure or restore to health

동 curative, healthful, medicinal, remedial, sanative

예 *healing powers of herbal remedies*

---

unfortunately [ʌnfɔ:rt ʃ ənətli]   불행하게도

图 by bad luck

동 dismally, lamentably, regrettably, unhappily, unluckily

예 *Unfortunately it rained all day.*

---

send [sénd]   보내다

图 cause to go somewhere

동 consign, direct, dispatch, ship, transmit

예 *The explosion sent the car flying in the air.*

nourish [nɛ:riʃ]   기르다

뜻 provide with nourishment

동 cherish, feed, foster, nurture, sustain

예 *This kind of food is not nourishing for young children.*

---

occasionally [əkéiʒənəli]   때때로

뜻 now and then or here and there

동 at times, from time to time, now and then, on occasion, sometimes

예 *He was arrogant and occasionally callous.*

---

leave [líːv]   떠나다

뜻 go away from a place

동 abscond, depart, escape, move, withdraw

예 *She didn't leave until midnight.*

---

afflict [əflíkt]   괴롭히다

뜻 cause great unhappiness for

동 aggrieve, ail, distress, plague, torment

예 *She was afflicted by the death of her parents.*

---

transportation [trɑnspərtéiʃən]   수송

뜻 the act of moving something from one location to another

동 carrying, conveyance, portage, traffic, transport

예 *means of transportation*

---

search [sɛ:rtʃ]   찾다

뜻 try to locate or discover, or try to establish the existence of

동 examine, investigate, ransack, rummage, seek

예 *The police are searching for clues.*

---

prediction [pridík ʃ ən]   예보, 예언

图 the act of predicting as by reasoning about the future

图 divination, forecast, prognosis, prognostication, prophecy

예 *make a prediction*

---

dare [dɛ̀ər]   도전하다

图 challenge

图 attempt, challenge, defy, try, venture

예 *I dare you!*

---

equip [ikwip]   갖추어 주다

图 provide with something usually for a specific purpose

图 accouter, attire, endow, fit, outfit

예 *The expedition was equipped with proper clothing, food, and other necessities.*

---

exposure [ikspóuʒər]   드러남

图 the state of being vulnerable or exposed

图 disclosure, display, exposition, revelation, uncovering

예 *his exposure to ridicule*

---

categorize [kǽtəgəràiz]   분류하다

图 place into or assign to a category

图 assort, class, classify, grade, sort

예 *Children learn early on to categorize.*

---

hardship [háːrd ʃ ìp]   곤란

图 a state of misfortune or affliction

图 adversity, difficulty, distress, privation, suffering

예 *Debt-ridden farmers struggling with hardship.*

---

vehicle [víːikl]   탈것

图 a conveyance that transports people or objects

통 car, carriage, conveyance, transport, wheels

예 *heavy goods vehicle*

---

estimation [èstəméiʃən]   판단

图 a judgment of the qualities of something or somebody

통 appraisal, esteem, evaluation, judgment, valuation

예 *In my estimation the boy is innocent.*